A BOND

ODYSSEY

ADAM MUCKLE

Copyright © 2024 by Adam Muckle

All rights reserved.

ABOUT THE AUTHOR

A lifelong Bond fan and a Classics graduate, Adam Muckle has been a professional tutor for over fifteen years. He is a Past President and Honorary Fellow of The Tutors' Association, the professional body for tutoring in the UK. By blending his dual interests of Classics and the James Bond franchise of books and films, his aim is to both educate and entertain his readers, leaving them shaken, not stirred.

CONTENTS

Foreword vii
Introduction ix

• PART I •
Themes

Bond as a Classical Hero 002
History and Legacy 009
East and West 019
Greece and Rome 024
Identity and Disguise 033
Xenia 042
Life and Death 046
Tragedy and Trilogy 053
Man and Myth 060

• PART II •
Miscellaneous Musings on the Classical Connections in Bond

Dr. No 068
From Russia With Love 072
Goldfinger 076
Thunderball 079
You Only Live Twice 082
On Her Majesty's Secret Service 087

Diamonds are Forever 089
Live and Let Die 091
The Man with the Golden Gun 094
The Spy Who Loved Me 096
Moonraker 098
For Your Eyes Only 099
Octopussy 101
A View to a Kill 105
The Living Daylights 107
Licence to Kill 112
Goldeneye 116
Tomorrow Never Dies 118
The World Is Not Enough 121
Die Another Day 124
Casino Royale 127
Quantum of Solace 130
Skyfall 132
Spectre 134
No Time to Die 136

Epilogue 139
For Further Reading 141
Acknowledgements 143

FOREWORD

The Pre-Title

You've been waiting at least two years, you've picked up every morsel of information of its pre-production, production and post-production from the internet, you've soaked up the hype. You've bought the tickets well in advance to get the first screening on the night of its release. You've come with friends or family in what has become tradition. You've bought the popcorn, the drinks. You may have extended the celebrations either side of the screening. You're maybe dressed to kill for the occasion. There's a bit of hustle and bustle as other people take their seats, too close for comfort for others. There's the overlong adverts, some decent trailers, perhaps too loud and too long. But the wait is almost over.

The curtains draw back, the screen widens and the auditorium gets darker. This is it. The film's rating classification appears followed by the studio logo. The MGM lion roars. Here we go.

DA-DA-DUM, DA-DA-DUM! The famous musical motif blasts. White dots on a black background move along the screen from left to right alongside dramatic pulsing theme music. An iris opens up to reveal an impeccably-tailored lone man walking across the silver screen from right to left. He turns to the camera and shoots directly at the frame, at you, at us, the audience.

Blood runs down the screen, the man and iris fade and the iris dot turns white, fading into a mysterious scene and an opening that could make the best film ever. Anticipation is high. A brand new Bond adventure. Together with audiences all around the world, we are more than ready to witness what lies in store for our hero. A Bond Odyssey.

INTRODUCTION

"Yesterday is a Memory. Today is History. Tomorrow is in the hands of one man." So announces the teaser trailer for *Tomorrow Never Dies* in early 1997. The anticipation, expectation and excitement for a new James Bond film roused once more for its release later in the year.

I was brought up on watching the Bond films, and a lot of other classic films beyond that. My father, stepfather and other father figures played their significant role in this boy's development towards manhood. They lit the spark. This seems to be a common entry-point for boys to get interested in the world of Bond. It's a rite of passage. It introduced cultural touchstones, a world of intrigue, danger and adventure, noble and ignoble character traits, good and evil, as well as aspects of History, Geography, Politics and social issues through the years. Each film in particular is a time capsule for social *mores*. Such things lead inquiring minds to other interests too, whether film, literature, music, travel and all the goodness life has to offer.

So I was a child of the '90s and already a Bond fan. When an Irish Celt was cast in the role of Bond, the cinematic experience of *Goldeneye* undoubtedly had a more profound impact on this twelve-year-old boy from Northern Ireland.

Having had my fill of children's literature, I was then keen to read Ian Fleming's novels - the Pan paperback editions which I read assiduously. I also loved the music, the sweeping soundtracks of John Barry and David Arnold and others, and collecting the Corgi cars. I wanted to find out as much as I could about the character, the books, the films; so much so that friends and family would say I now have an encyclopaedic knowledge. I enjoyed the detail and the trivia. I know this is not a unique experience. I was part of a new generation embracing this new wave of Bond as a cultural icon. Through the character's reinvention and adaptation with each new film and actor, each new audience can appreciate this timeless character, a hero for all time.

At the same time as *Goldeneye* was released, at a new school I was finding a flair for Latin and subsequently Greek. I was soaking up the languages like a sponge and subsequently studied it to undergraduate degree-level. As a Classicist who has translated and read the stories of Greek myth as well as the history of the Ancient Greeks, Romans and their civilisations, one can see their influence in modern times in a whole host of areas of our daily lives. In fact, for many who have studied Latin and/or Classical Greek begrudgingly, they only realise the language's significance years later. On that note, when you sit down to watch a modern film, the MGM logo appears with its motto *ARS GRATIA ARTIS*, Latin for *'art for the sake of art'*. Basically, entertainment for entertainment's sake. So now you know. Latin gives prestige and a bit of class and knowledge to various aspects of daily life.

I have been curious as to what classical influences were drawn from specifically for Bond. Moreover, as a tutor I would like to reveal these influences, making the unknown known and a new perspective for how we appreciate this character and the creativity of the franchise. So often in Bondology or other interests, we read what we already know rather than new information, whether big or small. So this book will focus on the classical influences on the world of Bond, whether they were intentional or not, it should add another layer of understanding.

Given their notoriety over the books, focus will be on the films. However, due attention will be given to the Ian Fleming, Kingsley Amis, John Gardner and Raymond Benson, Anthony Horowitz novels, and the other continuation authors where appropriate. It will also serve as an encouragement if you haven't had the pleasure of experiencing reading these yet. If I achieve anything from this book, it will be for you to have picked up the book in the first place, spark your curiosity and be inspired to read more.

The first part of the book will look at various themes running through the series while the second will focus on each film, from *Dr No* to *No Time to Die*, and study a particular aspect of the film and how it relates to ancient literature and/or life, as well as the rest of the series of films or books. In each it is a new way to discover and appreciate the series.

Surprisingly, the word 'school' comes from the Greek *scholē*, meaning 'leisure', the freedom to pursue knowledge.

Indeed in Latin there is also an etymological link with books - *libri* and freedom - *libertas* and the verb 'to free' - *liberare*. The word *liberi* - children also is connected. The Athenians sent their children to school to nurture their curiosity. So with that in mind, with this book I want to blend a hobby, an interest, an entertainment with some learning for you.

People see what they want to see when they pick up and look at something closely enough. It is understandably a subjective response. Everyone can find something different if they look hard enough. Sean Connery gave an interview for the BBC when filming *Diamonds Are Forever*, speaking of how people regard Bond, his approach to the character and the making of the films, he explained:

It's like if you've made something and you leave it a while, then someone picks it up, and everyone will pick it up, and see it as something else or look at it in a different way and I don't think there's anything you can do about it after you've done it.

I have read articles about Bond being a religion, about differing opinions about the first continuation novel *Colonel Sun*, about favourite Bond films being *Diamonds Are Forever* and *The Man with the Golden Gun*. Everyone's opinion and point of view can be respected. This franchise of films, books, comics, videogames and memorabilia have created so much content that it almost demands that. However, these are dependent on a person's entry point to Bond: who their first Bond actor was in what film they watched on the big screen, when they were introduced to the books, and who introduced them. I have my own favourites but I also hope I am level-headed and sober enough to bring some objectivity to proceedings as well. As M aptly recites Alfred - Lord - Tennyson's *Ulysses* in *Skyfall*, I will endeavour *"to strive, to seek, to find and not to yield."*

PART I
THEMES

Bond as a Classical Hero

It has been well-documented that Ian Fleming created the character of James Bond as a way to come to terms with his forthcoming marriage, to long for days of adventure and to form a new hero evoking all the qualities of a post-war, post-empire British hero for a new Elizabethan age.

Fleming imbued his protagonist with many qualities that the reader can find admirable, harking back to other literary and mythical classical heroes. A hero that can do things that the reader simply can't or won't do in day-to-day existence. This is pure escapist entertainment. We can be in another world through the eyes of our hero. Roger Moore, in a press interview for *The Spy Who Loved Me* during the opening of the new 007 Stage at Pinewood Studios on 5 December 1976, explained that this was the role of the Bond films for the audience:

Better that they should escape from their humdrum normal existence into the world of fantasy and relax. That's what entertainment means. The Greek theatre meant to transport the audience to the gods, which meant you let them see heaven, which is another way of saying to take oneself out of oneself.

Bond on this escapist stage is therefore larger than life. He shows strength, bravery and cunning. By definition he has legendary status like Achilles, Odysseus or Hector of Homer's epic narratives. The word *legend* comes from the Latin gerund; these heroes and epics are required to be read. The modern films have leaned into this in their narratives more and more, with their epic scale, budget and with longer running time.

These types of characters resonate deeply in the human experience, identifying with a character's behaviour or style whether in one's personal development growing up or as an adult. Films today such as *The Bourne Identity, Batman Begins, Man of Steel* or *Casino Royale* aren't just great films. They are films of characters discovering their own identity, where each audience member can find or reflect on their own.

The ancient heroes of Homer live and die in pursuit of honour, in pursuit of *kleos*, glory. They assert their greatness by the excellence and efficiency with which they kill. Their lives focus on fighting, whether in war or during an epic quest. They have special, unique talents and abilities which sets them apart from everyone else. In this dangerous world that they face, these individuals show conviction and courage. They persevere, show ingenuity and adaptability. They are determined and inspirational, with ingrained moral integrity of loyalty and honesty, with which they overcome their obstacles and get through their adventures.

One can see the parallels with Bond and other heroes, whether literary or cinematic. As Bruce Feirstein, the screenwriter for the first three Pierce Brosnan Bond films and numerous Bond videogames puts it:

Bond is an archetype that exists in every society. Going back to year zero, every culture has a myth in which the emperor sends a lone warrior to save a vanquished nation… The one man who can do it.

There is a certain debt owed to Joseph Campbell and his work *The Hero with a Thousand Faces*. First published in 1949, it is a study of comparative mythology discussing the theory of mythological structure and the journey of the archetypal hero found in most world myths. Hollywood filmmakers have become inspired by his writing and develop the Hero's Journey found in many stories. From leaving home, to being given a task to complete, seeking advice from mentors before facing various challenges in order to complete the task, the hero returns home having learnt something new, a more developed character. That is the Hero's Journey, reflecting in many ways our own life journeys.

The difference with Bond is that he is set up as an anti-hero. He has faults like all of us, which makes him more relatable. He is a tragic hero, an occasional narcissistic protagonist who is lacking in comparison to a conventional hero. The anti-hero can feel rejected by society and go down a self-destructive path leading to isolation or even death itself. Timothy Dalton has described Bond as a hero who murders in cold blood; Daniel Craig has said that Bond is more like a bad person on the side of good.

The Greek tragedians of the fifth century BC imbued the heroes of Homeric epic with this sense of hubris, excessive pride that blinds. This development in storytelling is what makes the more complex heroes interesting, and what has made Bond interesting and durable as a long-lasting character in popular culture. Fleming himself said, *"Presumably I am sufficiently in love with the myth to write basically incredible stories with a straight face."*

Henry Chancellor in the guide *James Bond: The Man and his World* sums up the story structures succinctly:

James Bond was St George, defender of the British Government (and the free world), who fights the dragon, named Goldfinger or Blofeld or Dr No - and - having slain him - then beds the girl. Perched on top of this mystical story was all the worldly know-how of cars, gadgets, food and gambling that Fleming corralled from his own experience.

In the publicity junket for *The Living Daylights* in 1987, Timothy Dalton described his approach to portraying the character and explaining the idea of a hero:

I didn't want to change the character. I wanted to try and bring to life, in this film The Living Daylights, the essence and spirit of James Bond, Ian Fleming's creation. I went straight to the books to discover what he'd written, to find Ian Fleming's James Bond. It struck me also that too many of our heroes today are called superheroes, blessed by a kind of magic, a supernatural quality that takes them away from real people. The real heroes come from us. There are men and women who in difficult circumstances can bring out some extraordinary human qualities. And that's the kind of Bond Fleming wrote about.

Twelve years later, Dalton's successor Pierce Brosnan while promoting *The World Is Not Enough,* at the Hong Kong Press Conference he was asked what is the essence of James Bond. He remarked:

Cruelty, vodka martinis, sex, his weapon. Because the man deals with killing and has a licence to kill. There is, you know, a dark side to him. Not that I want to make it that, but just when you have elements of it within the movie. It just makes him bigger. It makes him more of a hero. It makes him more accessible to the audience out there. They can identify with him, that there is this beating heart in there. And then you have all the wit and charm and the throwaway one-liners… the man is fallible. This man has feelings. He has doubts. And there's moral ambiguity there. And I think when you go into the grey area of any character, that's when you get interesting drama. It's in the books. Fleming does make this character fractured.

So modern day heroes are generally portrayed differently from ancient heroes and people have different expectations. To stay current and relevant, it is for the creators of the Bond franchise to not necessarily adapt Bond himself, but to adapt, like us, to the world around him and show how he responds to a changing world. This keeps things fresh, as has proven over sixty years and counting.

The Classical Villain

Antagonists are as much an archetype as the protagonist. The henchmen of the main villain pose a real physical threat to Bond and are themselves an archetype found in myth.

Arguably the first film embodiment is Red/Donald Grant played by Robert Shaw. He set such a precedent for the role of henchmen or supervillain, a physical equal to Bond that many of the later films seem to emulate, this Aryan-blonde, muscled character: Hans in *You Only Live Twice*, Kriegler in *For Your Eyes Only*, Necros in *The Living Daylights,* and Stamper in *Tomorrow Never Dies.*

Other giants include Oddjob, Tee Hee, Jaws, Hinx and Primo. They are real physical challengers who put Bond through his paces that it almost becomes a relief to him, and to the audience, when they finally meet their maker.

Sometimes it is the villain himself that poses as much a physical as well as intellectual threat to Bond: Dr No, Blofeld (in *On Her Majesty's Secret Service),* Largo, Mr Big/Kananga, Scaramanga, Zorin, Sanchez, Trevelyan, Gustav Graves and Silva would be characteristic of this.

These characters have some basis in Greek myth. The *Gigantes,* the Giants, were a race of great strength and aggression, though not necessarily of great size, not how we think of giants today. They battled the Olympian gods in the Gigantomachy. Archaic and Classical representations show them as militaristic and human in form. They were sometimes confused with the Titans and their own war with the Olympian gods, the Titanomachy.

The Giants were variously described by ancient authors: great-hearted, insolent, forward, strong and great. They were born *"with gleaming armour, holding long spears in their hands."* Others described them by their excesses, destroyed by hubris, *"they suffered unforgettable punishments for the evil they did."* Homer compared the Giants to the Laestrygonians, who *"hurled…rocks huge as a man could lift,"* possessing great strength, great size, their King's wife described as being as big as a mountain!

Some descriptions make the Giants less human, more monstrous, more gigantic, a frightening appearance, long hair, beards, scaly feet, serpent-footed, with a hundred arms or serpent-haired… Various visuals from Bond films may come to mind as to how diabolical attributes Bond's villains have been given. The Bond henchmen and more villains generally follow in this epic tradition from Greek myth.

The Gigantomachy represents victory of order over chaos, victory of divine order and rationalism of the Olympian gods over discord and excessive violence of the Giants. It was a victory of civilisation over barbarism. Plato compared it to a philosophical dispute about existence; Cicero described it as *"fighting against Nature"*, Lucretius as a victory of philosophy over mythology and superstition. Without labouring the point further, essentially Bond is the victor over the Giants of today.

History and Legacy

The World Is Not Enough

James Bond's family motto was first referenced in the novel *On Her Majesty's Secret Service* as the coat of arms of Sir Thomas Bond. Bond is doing cover research on heraldry for his next mission to ensnare Ernst Stavro Blofeld. Bond adopts the motto *orbis non sufficit - The World Is Not Enough* - as his own without seemingly much sentimentality.

However, for Bond's creator Ian Fleming, the bibliophile that he was, the supposed motto for his hero would surely have had greater significance and far more thought behind it. Indeed, its origin comes from possibly the greatest of historical figures in ancient times. The purported epitaph of Alexander the Great, related by the biographer Plutarch around 100 AD, over four hundred years after Alexander's death, happens to be *"A tomb now suffices for whom the world was not enough."* The link between Bond and this epic historical pseudo-mythic figure is therefore worthy of exploration.

Alexander did exist. He is a figure from history, a real man. However, there is as much myth in this man as there is history. These legendary accounts are largely from his own lifetime, likely encouraged by Alexander himself. One is that his mother Olympias was prophesied to bear a son who would be bold and lion-like. Another that his father Phillip's horse won three victories coinciding with Alexander's birth. When Alexander first tamed his famous steed Bucephalus, his father noted that Macedonia would not be large enough for his son.

Being Macedonian, his 'Greekness' would have been in question, not being a 'true' Hellene. He would have been considered in some ways an outsider. Like Bond having Celtic roots in Scotland, through the success of the books and film franchise, despite his fictional origin he has had a profound impact on British soft power and what we and the wider world consider 'British'.

Alexander became legendary as a classical hero in the mould of Achilles. This features prominently in historical and mythical traditions of both Greek and non-Greek cultures.

In terms of Alexander's character, he had unparalleled success as a military commander. He never lost a battle, despite often being outnumbered. He became personally involved in the battles he won. There is a fitting Greek word for describing Alexander in this way: *pothos*. The word means an unusually powerful longing for some unusually difficult goal. This links with his devotion to Homer and the ideal of such heroes as Achilles and Patroclus who continuously strive to be first and among the best. Having run out of mortal men to rival, it seems as though Alexander set himself to emulate heroes such as Heracles and even gods such as Dionysus. Perhaps he considered that nothing less than what was owed to his superhuman origins. His legacy is the Greeks' often extraordinary and still *potent* achievements.

When faced with opponents who used unfamiliar fighting techniques he adapted his approach accordingly. These are features unlikely to have passed by Fleming when creating his own hero. Bond is a man who always wins. The blending of what is real and what is myth with Alexander the Great is analogous perhaps to the Bond films using real world modern locations to add authenticity to the storytelling and the character of Bond himself.

Although nurtured by his father to be ambitious and by his mother to be aware of his destiny, Alexander did have a number of flaws. He had a violent temper, was rash and impulsive, which often influenced his decision-making. He was stubborn but open to reasoned debate. He also had a calmer side. He was logical and calculating, had a desire for knowledge, a love of philosophy and was an avid reader. He kept an encased copy of *The Iliad* with him on his travels, inspiring him to be a striving warrior, seeing himself and by others as a second Achilles. He was intelligent and was quick to learn, a quality instilled by his tutor Aristotle.

However, he had a lack of self-control with alcohol. It could be argued that Alexander brought upon his own early death at thirty-two by drinking a separate toast to each of his twenty dinner guests one by one and finishing off a twelve-pint pitcher of wine. The orator Demosthenes (384-322) remarked that *"having a drink is an excellent quality in a sponge but not a king."*

Alexander had great charisma, seeking ideals of honour (*timè*) and glory (*kudos*). However, in his final years,

Alexander was exhibiting signs of megalomania and paranoia. These are perhaps characteristics Fleming likely drew on for Bond as well as his villains, with their delusions of grandeur and boundless ambition.

So much for the man but more on the motto. The phrase *orbis non sufficit* is thought to originate from the *Pharsalia* by Lucan. It appears twice, in reference to a group of villainous mutineers and to the ambitions of Julius Caesar. It was then applied to Alexander the Great by the comic poet Juvenal in his *Satires*: *"The world was not big enough for Alexander the Great, but a coffin was."*

As we glean from *On Her Majesty's Secret Service*, Bond Street in Westminster is named after Sir Thomas Bond, 1st Baronet, an English landowner and Comptroller of the household of Queen Henrietta Maria. He was created Baronet on 9th October 1658 by Charles II before the Restoration of the monarchy in 1660. His coat of arms is an argent on a Chevron sable with three bezants. The crest is a winged demi-horse, ensigned with six starts. It is recorded as being part of the window in St Giles, Camberwell which was destroyed in a fire in the nineteenth century. As for the motto, *non sufficit orbis* was used previously by Phillip II of Spain, with a medal struck in 1583 bearing the inscription.

The Birth of Bond

The first Bond novel was published on 13th April 1953. The date 13th April is included in his passport for the

2008 film *Quantum of Solace,* along with Daniel Craig's year of birth, as a nod to this landmark date for the character. In a way this could be considered his 'birth'day in the real world.

It is noteworthy too that 53 is a significant number for the creatives behind Bond. In *Dr No*, when pressed by Doctor No that it would be a pity to break the bottle of Dom Perignon '55, Bond responds arrogantly that he prefers the '53 himself. That is surely a nod to the literary Bond's emergence in *Casino Royale* in 1953. I would not be surprised if the release of *Casino Royale* in 2006 was almost a deliberate coincidence rather than choosing the once in a millennium opportunity of 2007 to mark the secret agent's signature number. The number 53 appears on the locker key for Dimitrios whom Bond is following at the BodyWorld exhibition, as another blink-and-you-miss-it nod to the literary creation.

However, as a character within his own universe he has been given the date of birth as 11th November 1920 by John Pearson in his 'official' biography, though 1924 is suggested by M's obituary for him, and 1921 has also been suggested. Regardless of the precise year of his birth, 11th November is Armistice Day, Remembrance Day, an important date for the British public and around the world. However, Fleming himself was vague, perhaps deliberately, about the character's actual age.

Bond's obituary published in *The Times* towards the end of the novel *You Only Live Twice* gives us some breadcrumbs of a backstory to the character.

He was born half-Scots, half-Swiss, and with his early education entirely abroad he inherited a *"first-class command"* of French and German. Both his parents, Andrew Bond and Monique Delacroix were killed in a climbing accident near Chamonix and he then became under the guardianship of his Aunt Charmian living with her in Pett Bottom, Kent. Bond then went to the public school Eton in Windsor but his time there was *"brief and undistinguished"* and after *"some alleged trouble with one of the boys' maids"* his aunt was *"requested to remove him."* He was then able to enter his father's old school Fettes in Edinburgh:

Here the atmosphere was somewhat Calvinistic, and both academic and athletic standards were rigorous. Nevertheless, though inclined to be solitary by nature, he established some firm friendships among the traditionally famous athletic circles at the school. By the time he left, at the early age of seventeen, he had twice fought for the school as a light-weight and had, in addition, founded the first serious judo class at a British public school.

Some claim that Fleming gave Bond Scottish lineage as a response to Sean Connery's casting. However, correspondence dating back to 1960 proves that Fleming had contacted a Scottish nobleman to help develop Bond's family history, in particular seeking a Scottish "Bond" family line, similar to the Flemings' own connections.

At these private schools of Eton, Fleming's old school, and Fettes College, with their worldwide reputations, young James would have received a very classical education. The word 'classical' or 'classics' comes from the Latin word *'classis'* meaning 'fleet'. So a whole fleet of subjects is taught. He would have learned the traditional subjects of English, Maths and the Sciences but also Latin, Classical Greek, History and Geography. He would have been taught how to learn and how to think for himself, to broaden his horizons. He would have learnt about the roots of Western civilisation, the Greek and Roman myths, art and architecture, the natural sciences, inventions and developments in a whole host of areas.

He would also have learned among peers from all over the world, who would become leaders in the world in a variety of areas of life. So already he would be a well-cultured person and aware of the world around him. As today there would have been plenty of opportunities to take part in extracurricular activities, as evidenced by his founding the judo class. So even though his school career may have been *"brief and undistinguished"* he would still have received the very best possible learning environment that British education could have offered.

With the outbreak of war and fighting under age he reached the rank of Commander and part of the Royal Naval Volunteer Reserve, joining Naval Intelligence and quickly recruited for the Secret Service:

By now it was 1941 and, by claiming an age of nineteen and with the help of an old Vickers colleague of his father, he entered a branch of what was subsequently to become the Ministry of Defence. To serve the confidential nature of his duties, he was accorded the rank of lieutenant in the Special Branch of the R.N.V.R., and it is a measure of the satisfaction his services gave to his superiors that he ended the war with the rank of Commander.

Bond lives in a flat off King's Road, Chelsea. As noted by John Pearson in his Authorised Biography of 007, the flat is located at 30 Wellington Square. Fleming himself mentions Bond's flat in *Moonraker, From Russia with Love* and *Thunderball*. He describes it as *"the ground floor of a Regency house in a small Chelsea Square with Plane trees."* Wellington Square is a fitting abode for Bond for there is an instant connection with the British military hero Arthur Wellesley, the Duke of Wellington and his iconic British victory over Napoleon at Waterloo at the height of its imperial power.

As a side note, not far from Wellington Square on the other side of King's Road is Markham Square where Bond's flat may have resided. This explains the pseudonym *Robert Markham* used by Kingsley Amis for authoring *Colonel Sun* and, at that time, it had been proposed by Glidrose (now Ian Fleming Publications) for the authors of subsequent continuation novels.

In *Spectre*, the exterior of Bond's flat is not a square off the King's Road but at 1 Stanley Gardens, Notting Hill on the corner of Stanley Gardens and Stanley Crescent, with the entrance at Stanley Crescent. I guess MI6 did indeed sell his flat when they thought he was dead at the beginning of *Skyfall*. The spartan decor to the interior of the flat in *Spectre* certainly suggests so.

Aside from this brief background, as with so many heroes, we the audience, readers, as individuals are to project ourselves into the shoes of the protagonist and go on the journey with him. We can investigate his background and

• A BOND ODYSSEY •

what makes him tick. However, we already know enough to travel with him. The point is that what we don't know about him doesn't matter. That's the mystery. We are all searching for who we are. We go on the journey with the hero. This makes Bond relatable, this is what made Homer's heroes relatable.

In John Pearson's *James Bond: The Authorised Biography* there is a novel conceit that our fictional hero is a real man, a real intelligence officer and a real friend of Fleming. As requested by the British Secret Service, Fleming merely magnified this man Bond and his adventures for his novels to outwit the Soviets during the Cold War. This is alluded to with a knowing wink to the reader towards the end of Bond's obituary:

The inevitable publicity, particularly in the foreign press, accorded some of these adventures, made him, much against his will, something of a public figure, with the inevitable result that a series of popular books came to be written around him by a personal friend and former colleague of James Bond. If the quality of these books, or their degree of veracity, had been any higher, the author would certainly have been prosecuted under the Official Secrets Act. It is a measure of the disdain in which these fictions are held at the Ministry, that action has not yet — I emphasise the qualification — been taken against the author and publisher of these high-flown and romanticised caricatures of episodes in the career of an outstanding public servant.

"History is always then, myth is now," wrote the novelist Pat Barker. Myths exist to be reread, rewritten, reinterpreted.

We discover more about our hero and about ourselves, about the human condition, in these stories. That makes the interpretations of Bond's character by different actors and different media, whether given a lighter mood or more serious tone, so malleable throughout the years and given the series its longevity.

East and West

"East, West: points on the compass both as stupid as each other."

In Bond's first big-screen adventure *Dr No,* when Bond and Honey reach Dr No's lair on Crab Key and finally meet the man himself for dinner, the hero and villain discuss the nature of power and who holds power in the world. Bond is surprised that Dr No isn't working for the East. When his adversary says that East and West are just points on the compass, Bond realises the real risk of instability in world politics that Dr No and the organisation he represents could cause.

In sociology, the dichotomy of East and West is the difference between two cultural worlds rather than just geography. In the context of the Cold War, Dr No is talking politically.

This attitude of a world divided originated with the historian Herodotus writing in the fifth century BC, coming up with the terms "Asia" and "Europe". This contrast is still alive today. Herodotus was explaining the reasons for the Persian Wars between the Greeks and Persians. A film such as *300*, recounting the tale of King Leonidas' Spartan resistance in 478BC is relatable because of this opposition between Eastern and Western forces.

ie tragedy *Persae* (Persians) by Aeschylus in 472BC, Persia was identified as Asia. Herodotus states that the distinction begins with the Greek sack of Troy and climaxing with the Achaemenid invasions. This is when East/West became political, cultural and ideological rather than geographical. They became rival spheres. This is the defining theme of Herodotus' work and the theme entered the zeitgeist of the fifth century BC and from then on. The West is typically framed as enlightenment and progress, the East as tyranny and darkness.

This is clearly not how Doctor No sees it. He thinks both sides just as stupid as each other, and SPECTRE (*Special Executive for Counterintelligence, Terrorism, Revenge and Extortion*) a far superior organisation to play each off against each other and seal ultimate world domination. "Same old dream," says Bond. However, by making the enemy SPECTRE rather than the Soviet agency SMERSH, the filmmakers showed great foresight that their hero was much more than a Cold War hero. They rightly stayed out of politics, keeping Bond a hero for all in the long-run and thereby making their audience as wide as possible, regardless of any one political context.

Furthermore, the display of British power demonstrates the influence of the West in international affairs. Since its political status was diminished by the Second World War, its influence over the Americans is received by audiences with more acceptance by a global audience. Bond plays a diplomatic, peace-keeping role between East and West, as do the films themselves.

Moreover, it is not only Commander Bond himself that we see this role. The navy ships or Marines dispatched in the climax or aftermath of an adventure play their part in resolving international conflict. This is another trope that the series will harken back to moving forward, most prominently in *The Spy Who Loved Me, Goldeneye, Tomorrow Never Dies* and *No Time to Die*.

This foresight of Britain's role in international affairs and using its soft power to influence events has allowed Bond to be reinvented for the post-Cold War era. In *Goldeneye*, Bond symbolically blasts through a wall in St Petersburg, Russia with a T55 tank, symbolic of the breakdown of the Berlin Wall and the Soviet Union; the post-9/11 retrocon with *Casino Royale* starts a new timeline for a new era of geopolitics.

Even the continuation novels have managed to reinvent Bond for new relevant adventures, with John Gardner resurrecting the character for *Licence Renewed* and a new series of books for the '80s and early '90s, Raymond Benson placing his first Bond novel *Zero Minus Ten* in contemporary Hong Kong of 1997 and the time of its handover to China. Jeffrey Deaver's *Carte Blanche* attempted a completely new background for the character of Bond and a new history for a post-9/11 world before returning to the original Fleming timeline and 1967 for the next novel in William Boyd's *Solo*.

Bond can stay modern even though the world around him may change. It will be seen again with a future incarnation with a new actor.

Istanbul: Gateway to the East

To date the city of Istanbul has appeared in three Bond films: *From Russia With Love, The World Is Not Enough* and *Skyfall*. In each the location is central to the plot.

In *From Russia With Love*, the city serves very much as a gateway from East to West, from the Soviet Union to Western Europe. Bond muses to Moneypenny, Istanbul is "where the moonlight on the Bosphorus is irresistible." Istanbul in the film is SPECTRE's playground for playing off the Russians, Bulgars and British against one another, all in pursuit of a Lektor decoder, the MacGuffin of the plot. Through Bond's adventure we get a taste of the culture of Istanbul, its people, its architecture, its rich history, the food, drink… and Turkish dancing. Moreover, especially in these early films of the 60s as when the books were first published in the 50s, Britain and the rest of the world was coming out of post-war rationing and a time where international travel was a luxury. The notion of these films being travelogues can be embraced by the audience then as much as they can be today.

In *Licence to Kill* we learn from M that Bond should have been in Istanbul had it not been for his personal vendetta to avenge his friend Felix Leiter. It is not until a decade later that we see the film location again. *The World Is Not Enough* explores the influence of the Bosphorus for the trade traffic of oil pivotal for the future of the West's oil-supply.

"Not enough excitement in Istanbul?"

In *Skyfall*, Istanbul becomes a focal point for finding a list of spies pivotal to the West's security. Bond and Eve have to recover a stolen disk with the names and identities of British agents around the world. However, one could also see the opening scene as a message for the audience that Bond isn't just for Western audiences. The location and positioning of an international capital, Istanbul itself is a symbol for Bond's international appeal. The filmmakers were also looking East to China, as signposted by Shanghai later in the film, for a wider audience, recognising the region's growing influence in real world politics.

Istanbul mixes the tradition of the Byzantine and Ottoman empires with the modernity of a contemporary European city. It is very much the old with the new. In 1955, while covering an Interpol conference for The Sunday Times, Fleming stayed at the Istanbul Hilton. He describes Istanbul as *"a town the centuries had so drenched in blood and violence that, when daylight went out, the ghosts of its dead were its only population."* It was a town Bond *"would be glad to get out of alive."*

However, Cubby Broccoli in his biography *When the Snow Melts* described Fleming during his time visiting the set of the film *From Russia with Love* in 1962: *"He loved the sounds, the spicy smells, the bazaars, the street merchants and the belly dancers. Especially the belly dancers."*

By its very position on the world map, Istanbul's role in history is unique and allows for a great deal of cultural exchange. Bond thrives on and breaks down these geographical boundaries and politics of the day for the audience.

Greece and Rome

Greece and Greek Islands

Bond had visited Greece in a literary capacity before in Kingsley Amis' *Colonel Sun,* the author astutely acknowledging the fact that Fleming had not taken him there through his globetrotting. With its ancient and mythic past, there is a treasure-trove of classical allusions and inspirations to explore.

The most obvious is that of the Bond girl of the novel, Ariadne, her name evoking the Theseus and Minotaur myth. In the myth, Ariadne falls in love with Theseus, giving him a thread to find his way out from the labyrinth having killed the Minotaur. Theseus then flees with Ariadne, abandoning her on Dia, modern day Naxos.

So there are subtle allusions of the myth in the plot of the novel. However, Amis plays around with them. Bond is rescuing M, not Ariadne, the villain Sun is the Minotaur, the deception of boat- switching from *The Altair* to *The Cynthia* is much like the sails that are hoisted to signify whether Theseus is alive or dead, but Ariadne here is a strong independently-minded spy rather than the cypher of the Greek myth.

"From the air, Vrakonisi looks like the blade of a sickle drawn by a very drunk man."

Amis plays on the idea of Greek myth by placing his villain and the kidnapped M on an invented Greek island, Vrakonisi - Dragon Island - which one could place between Paros, Naxos and Ios, according to Amis himself in his 1991 introduction to the novel. Bond would have to get to the island, via Athens and fishing boat, allowing him - and thereby the reader - the opportunity to explore the best foods and culture that Greece has to offer, the Acropolis with its Parthenon, *"the best olives, the best shellfish, the best local wine, and the sun, the sea and the islands."* And ouzo for good measure. Bond reflects on the myths and foundations of ancient times with the post-war Americanisation of Greek culture: the crucible of Western civilisation embracing the ways of modern Western society. Very much a meeting of two worlds which tourists meet when they themselves might visit Greece.

"Ouzo for me, please."

Over a decade later, early treatments of the 1981 film *For Your Eyes Only*, the writers considered Bond visiting Athens and its Parthenon, inspired by his literary visit in *Colonel Sun*. However, being set in Greece, one cannot help notice a plethora of Greek influence in the story.

For a start, the name of the Bond girl, Melina, means honey in Ancient Greek, in a way a throwback to the

Honey of *Dr No*. Melina is on a personal mission of revenge for the death of her parents. She states that all Greek women, like Electra, *"always avenge their loved ones."* Electra is one of the most popular mythological characters in tragedy. She is the main character in two Greek tragedies of the fifth century BC: *Electra* by Sophocles and *Electra* by Euripides. She is also the central figure in Aeschylus' plays as well: she is regarded as a vengeful soul in *The Libation Bearers*, the second play in the playwright's Oresteia trilogy.

Along with her brother Orestes, she plotted matricidal revenge against their mother Clytemnestra and Aegisthus for the murder of their father Agamemnon.

When Bond is captured by Columbo onto his yacht and they meet for the first time, Columbo praises Bond for what the Greeks call *thrasos* - guts. If one delves deeper, there is another insight here into Bond's character. Although the word *thrasos* itself can be used to mean courage and boldness it can also be interpreted and translated as over-boldness or insolence, bordering on hubris.

In the only instance where *thrasos* appears as a personification, in Aeschylus' *Agamemnon,* it is a malicious and suspicious being as opposed to a more virtuous trait. That is the line that Bond or others in his profession walk, between the shades of light and dark, between right and wrong. It takes guts to do so. Bond proves his *thrasos* when toppling Locque off the cliff-edge in revenge for Luici Ferrara and Countess Lisl who have already helped him on his mission.

• A BOND ODYSSEY •

"Are we in the twentieth century or in ancient Greece?"

In Raymond Benson's third Bond adventure, following on from *Zero Minus Ten* and the film novelisation of *Tomorrow Never Dies*, *The Facts of Death* was published in 1998. Originally it had been intended to be titled *The World Is Not Enough,* but this mantle was taken the following year by the entitled Bond film. However, the last chapter bears Bond's motto.

In the novel Bond is in Cyprus where a number of British troops have been discovered murdered in mysterious circumstances. All these and following deaths are connected as near all the bodies were statues of Greek deities and numbers.

The prime suspect is an international mathematical cult called the Decada, its head being Konstantinos Romanos, the Monad, the One. He believes he is on a mission from the Greek gods who he claims speak to him, and that the soul of Pythagoras lives within him.

Bond beats Romanos in a game of baccarat in Athens and the villain is subsequently killed by another member of the Decada, femme fatale Hera Volopoulos. The plot is to start a major war between Greece and Turkey, with Hera wishing to release a virus and ransom the world with its vaccine.

I remember vividly being struck by how many Classical Greek influences there were in the novel. So much so that I shared the book with my Classics Master who read it overnight, finding it a real page-turner.

The book is packed with classical references, initially from the Ancient Agora of Athens, Hera, Poseidon, the characteristics of the Greek gods, the dead on their journey with the ferryman Charon on the River Styx to Hades. And that's just at the beginning. The island of Chios with its visitors and inhabitants such as Jason, Homer and the mathematician and philosopher Pythagoras is also identified.

In the villainous organisation's secret meeting, the Monad speaks of the deaths to the group:

"The gods are pleased," he said. "Our first tribute was to the ancient Greeks, who built the Agora in Athens at the base of the holy Acropolis. We owe our allegiance to these ancestors of all mankind. It was in Greece where true western thought materialised. They built the Temple of Hephaisteion, where Zeus and the other gods of Mount Olympus were worshiped, and it was there that we left out little… sacrifice. Our second tribute was to Hera, Queen of the Gods. The third was to Poseidon, god of the sea and brother of Zeus. Our fourth was to Ares, the god of war."

When Bond arrives in Athens, met by Greek Secret Service agent Niki Mirakos, Bond notes that she says *Hellas,* the Greek word for Greece. Bond reflects that he is not fluent in Greek. "*He could read it, but couldn't speak it, except for some common words and expressions.*"

As he checks into his hotel, the Hotel Grande Bretagne in Constitution Square, he remembers staying there during the Colonel Sun affair, a nice nod to the Kingsley Amis

Bond book. The foyer contains a *"good copy of a Gobelins tapestry featuring Alexander the Great entering Babylon."*

Through Niki, Bond discovers that Romanos was a noted author and one of the most brilliant mathematicians in the Western World and is extremely wealthy, a gambler and leader of a spiritual and philosophical organisation called the New Pythagorean Society. He owns a big yacht called the *Persephone* that sails all over the Aegean. For those who don't know, Persephone is the daughter of Zeus and Demeter who is seized by Hades to be queen of the Underworld. Later in the novel, it is revealed that the entire ship is a stage setting for a Greek tragedy by Aeschylus or Euripides, the whole interior of the ship being in the style of an ancient Greek galley.

As another subtle allusion to *Colonel Sun* and its character Ariadne, the Theseus myth is related to Bond by Niki when they learn of another dead body. King Aegeas threw himself into the sea and died when Theseus hadn't changed the sails on his boat to show his mission from Crete to rescue Ariadne and kill the Minotaur was a success. That sea is now called the Aegean and the Temple of Poseidon was built there in his memory.

Benson also relates the myth of Agamemnon, his murderous wife Clytemnestra and his kingdom Mycenae, when a kidnapped Bond approaches Mount Agios Ilias and Mount Zara. Both their tombs are located in the ruin of Mycenae. This morbidity adds to the ominous tone of the scene.

In the last chapter of the book, *The World Is Not Enough*, where he reveals his family motto to Niki, she replies that he is not like other men:

"You are human, but you have done superhuman things. All men know the facts of life, but you know just as much about the facts of death! You have thwarted Death many times.... In ancient Greece, men would have proclaimed you to be a god. You would have been another Jason or an Agamemnon or even an Alexander the Great. There would be statues of you on display throughout the country and in museums!"

As well as adding to the story of the man, Benson is contributing to the legend. Bond is indeed a modern day equivalent of one of these epic heroes. The placing of Bond in a Greek landscape emphasises this. It also adds a didactic element. It enriches the reader in learning about Greek myth and Greece's history and culture while accompanying Bond on his adventure.

Rome

It is the Italian idyllic scenery that plays its part in the Bond films in which the country features.

It first appears in *From Russia With Love* in Venice with a decisive chess match and in the aftermath of what Bond believes is the end of his mission, only to come face to face with Rosa Klebb with her deadly footwear and allow her to *'have her kicks'*. We see Bond and Tatiana Romanova in a standard Venice setting, on a gondola as the credits roll.

• A BOND ODYSSEY •

It takes over a decade for us to see Bond in Italy again. In *The Spy Who Loved Me* Bond and his Soviet counterpart Anya Amasova are in Sardinia investigating shipping magnate Karl Stromberg. The island provides the forum for Bond's exciting car chase with his Lotus Esprit. We see Bond in Venice again in *Moonraker* with its glass industry playing a prominent role in the plot as well as for an extreme boat chase along the Grand Canal with Bond's gondola turned hovercraft traversing St Mark's Square.

We see Italy in winter in *For Your Eyes Only* in Cortina d'Ampezzo, the venue for the 1956 Winter Olympics.

It isn't until the Daniel Craig era that we see it again: in Venice and Lake Como in *Casino Royale,* in Lake Garda and Carrara, Siena and other parts of Tuscany in *Quantum of Solace*, to the car chase in Vatican City, Rome in *Spectre* and the picturesque Matera and Puglia in *No Time to Die.*

Aside from the much discussed nighttime car chase in Rome climaxing along the Tiber river, there are other areas of the city worthy of note in *Spectre*. Mario Sciarra's funeral was filmed at the Museum of Roman Civilisation in the south of Rome. His widow Lucia Sciarra, played by Monica Bellucci is at Villa di Fiorano, on the Via Appia Antica less than two miles from Rome airport Ciampino. The mysterious SPECTRE meeting filmed at Blenheim Palace near Oxford, England, was likely inspired by the Royal Palace of Caserta. Given Bond's drive in his Aston Martin as he leaves Lucia, the meeting seems to take place on the Janiculum Hill.

However, despite the influence of the Roman Empire in history, the Bond films don't lean into this aspect of Italy, instead the finer aspects of style and culture of Italian living. Noone can ever doubt the sheer beauty of Italian landscapes.

Italy's ancient past or landscape is not a remarkable aspect of the literary Bond either, more a happenstance. In the collection of short stories, *For Your Eyes Only,* the fourth short story, *Risico,* sees Bond in Italy where he meets his contact Kristatos. He points him towards the smuggler Colombo. In order to get to Colombo, Bond wines and dines his mistress Lisl Baum. When Colombo reveals to Bond that he has been deceived, that it is in fact Kristatos who is the Soviet smuggler to investigate, not him.

Rome was one of Fleming's least favourite cities and Bond himself therefore seems to also have little interest in the city beyond the food and drink. He makes no effort to see the Colosseum nor the nearby Roman forum, as the majority of people visiting Rome would likely do.

Identity and Disguise

Bond: a modern-day Dionysus

At university I wrote an essay on the Greek god Dionysus, the Roman god Bacchus. He is the god of fertility, wine and pleasure. That is just the beginning of where we can make some clear connections between this divine classical character from ancient myth and our modern-day British hero.

In Greek myth Dionysus circumnavigates the globe by boat or winged chariot, charming and influencing those he comes into contact. Sound familiar? Bond travels in many different modes but is most recognisable with his Aston Martin DB5, its logo coincidentally being a pair of wings. In the books, his trusted Bentley also has a winged emblem.

Dionysus shares the secrets of wine-making in the same way Bond would share his specifications of the perfect vodka martini or other beverage. All this drinking seems to have no significant effect on Dionysus nor to Bond, in contrast to his followers, us mere mortals. Bond is considered the best shot in the Service despite his excessive drinking.

In terms of accoutrements, Dionysus carries a *thyrsus*, a sacred pinecone tipped staff wreathed in vines. It is a phallic symbol often displayed with a wine-cup denoting female sexuality. The pinecone and the vine formed a symbol of fertility and rebirth, with an iron tip in its point to make a weapon. Bond is no stranger to weaponry and the element of surprise. He may use his Walther PPK in a hidden holster but also day-to-day items from Q Branch, whether it be a pair of glasses to trigger a bomb, an attaché case with hidden lethal tricks or an explosive Parker Pen. Alongside his weapon he of course may be seen with his signature vodka martini, shaken not stirred.

In terms of rebirth and resurrection, each film reintroduces Bond, no matter what the circumstance we last saw him. In *Skyfall* he is resurrected after being shot by Moneypenny and falls off the bridge into the river seemingly dead. Thematically, he will become reborn. In *No Time to Die,* we see him actually die. But, with these classical links in the pantheon of the gods and heroes of myth, we can trust that he will be back to fight another day.

Dionysus is a god of intoxication and ecstasy, representing the surrender of everyday activity. He is attractive to his female followers, the Maenads, whom he lures into an ecstatic frenzy. Bond likewise brings either divine ecstasy in bed or brutal death to his foes. A perfect example of this can be seen in the film *Dr No*, when Bond arrives at Miss Taro's house. The audience is not sure as Bond tightens the towel in his hands whether he is going to kill her or seduce her.

Dionysus is frequently represented as youthful, almost effeminate, with luxuriant hair, relaxing with grapes, wine-cup in hand, or holding his *thyrsus*. In a similar way, the typical image of Bond could be considered in some ways a modern-day Dionysus: a man depicted in the prime of his life in his thirties or forties, pristine, well-groomed and suave without a hair out of place.

Moreover, Dionysus is the god of drama, lending his name to the first theatrical festivals for playwrights of tragedy, comedy and satyr plays in Athens in the fifth century BC, the Dionysia. Perhaps the spirit of Dionysus breathes through the Bond films in the movie theatres, containing as they do different blends of serious drama, emotion and light comedy depending on the era in which they are released and what trends are occurring in the cinema landscape at the time. *Dr No* is a very different beast to *Moonraker* and attracts a different audience while carrying an existing audience. Dionysus is seemingly a god for everyone with wide appeal.

Today, our escapist hero Bond is ready for action, taking his audience with him on his next globe- trotting adventure, giving joy and thrills to an audience of millions around the world.

Disguise

We find out the most about the god Dionysus in literature in one of Euripides's final plays, *The Bacchae*. The god returns to his paternal home of Thebes to punish the king Pentheus for not giving proper respect to him. He comes disguised and slowly but surely through the narrative his identity is revealed before it is all too late for Pentheus.

Disguise and infiltration have become a staple of literature. Odysseus disguises himself as a beggar when he returns to his home to regain his authority, his wife and place as King of Ithaca. Disguise is all part of the Hero's Journey.

Like Dionysus toying with Pentheus, in *Die Another Day* the antagonist Colonel Tan-Sun Moon goes to the greatest lengths to disguise his identity to the world: DNA therapy to transform himself from an Asian Korean into a Caucasian English aristocratic millionaire. While it may not pass the political correctness police of today, it does set up much dramatic irony when he encounters Bond at Blades, who is completely oblivious of ever meeting him before.

Although he himself doesn't like physical disguises, Bond will often infiltrate an organisation or party in disguise in order to extract information and develop the plot:

- Mr Fisher in *You Only Live Twice*

- Sir Hilary Bray in *On Her Majesty's Secret Service*

- Peter Franks in *Diamonds are Forever*

- all in black in *Goldfinger, Thunderball* or *Live and Let Die*

- Scaramanga in *The Man with the Golden Gun*

- Marine biologist Robert Sterling in *The Spy Who Loved Me*

• A BOND ODYSSEY •

- a travel writer in *For Your Eyes Only*

- a South American colonel, circus performer, gorilla and clown in *Octopussy*

- an English aristocrat and financial journalist in *A View to a Kill*

- a friend of a Russian general in *The Living Daylights*

- infiltrating Sanchez's operations in *Licence to Kill*

- an investment banker in *Tomorrow Never Dies*

- a Russian nuclear physicist in *The World is not Enough*

- a diamond smuggler and an ornithologist in *Die Another Day*

- a short-lived disguise of professional gambler Arlington Beech in *Casino Royale*

- Robert Sterling again in *Quantum of Solace*

- a chauffeur in *Skyfall*

- an insurance broker in *Spectre*

- while infiltrating a SPECTRE birthday party for Blofeld, up until then he was trying to shed his role as a spy and assassin for a quieter normal life, but all in vain in *No Time to Die*.

"He's keen to get home."

Similar to the theme of rebirth and resurrection, *nostos* is a theme used in Ancient Greek literature, often cited when an epic hero returns home, often by sea. Indeed, it is where we get the word *nostalgia*: the psychological condition of longing for the past.

The James Bond franchise as a series is in many ways built and reliant on nostalgia. That feeling of connection with memorable moments of our lives and sharing it with others to make connections in society. Each film, each book, each piece of memorabilia taps into that feeling. For my part, I especially remember watching Bond films on television with family, each new Bond film with various family members and friends, and events surrounding each new film. They are snapshots in time of my life experience, as others will be for you. Although not necessarily the best, a particular film will contribute to whether they are favourites, as they are personal to me. That's nostalgia in action.

Nostos is a key theme in many aspects of *The Odyssey* but mainly to describe Odysseus' own journey back home from Troy after twenty years' absence from his wife: ten years fighting at Troy and ten years of effort to reach home. It was deemed a high level of heroism or greatness for those who managed to return. The journey is usually very extensive and includes being shipwrecked in an unknown location and going through certain trials that can test the hero, retaining or elevating their identity and status upon arrival.

• A BOND ODYSSEY •

In *Skyfall* we see a return to form for the Bond franchise on its golden anniversary on Her Majesty's Diamond Jubilee year. We also see Bond returning to active duty after his presumed death after the pre-title sequence, with M writing up his obituary in a dark and soused London.

We find Bond washed up on a distant Mediterranean island. One could argue that the Mediterranean woman he is with is Calypso-like, preventing his return. However, when Bond hears news of MI6 under attack and its headquarters bombed, this triggers his recall home to London to be of service to the realm once again. And like Odysseus returning home from Troy, in modern day Turkey, Bond having started in Istanbul, Turkey, he also finds it time to return home.

Therefore his first *nostos* is his return from a fall from grace. In Bond's case the fall is a literal one too, falling off a rail bridge and going AWOL, presumed dead. There is then a reconciliation and a gradual mending of his spirit.

There is also a metaphorical *nostos*: the true nature of his soul is returned to him bit-by-bit. Bond is stripped of his home, his identity and recognition by M. He is given a signature gun by Q when back on active service, akin to Odysseus regaining control being the only man to string his own bow in *The Odyssey* against the suitors. He is given a radio with an alert signal to receive rescue. Whenever Bond has scrubbed up and is given a traditional shave by Eve, he is ready for action. He has returned to form. He is once again in his dinner jacket, 100% dressed to kill, on board a skiff transporting him to the casino in

Macau, fireworks exploding behind him in the night sky almost in celebration; the bars of the James Bond theme in joyful synchronicity. Bond is back.

Skyfall was Bond's physical home but also representative of his childhood. His father's old shotgun is symbolic of this past life. Before blowing the house to smithereens he says, *"I always hated this place."* Bond is uncomfortable with the idea of home. He is a liminal, nomadic character who lives out of a suitcase; like Odysseus, he is a traveller; he is a British export rarely seen for long in his own homeland. The film plays with this idea on what is Bond's home: is it Britain, is it London, is it MI6, is it Scotland, is it Skyfall? Is he homeless, or is he just home less than the rest of us?

Past films have pondered where Bond would call home, showing his residences in *Dr No* and *Live and Let Die*. In *On Her Majesty's Secret Service* he suggests Belgrave Square to start a home with Tracy. In *No Time to Die* 'home' is Norway, Madeline's home where Bond's daughter also dwells, though unknown to him. At the beginning of the film, Bond's retirement home is Jamaica as well as it being the location for the creative genesis for the character himself by Fleming. When Felix dies, this is the trigger for Bond suited and booted with his renewed Aston Martin Vantage, to leave for London and MI6, his other home. The Bond theme audaciously announces his arrival that he is back in action.

One could argue that there is a second *nostos* for Bond in *Skyfall*. He finally returns 'home' to MI6 at the end of the film, reporting for duty 'with pleasure' to a new M, having undergone many trials through the course of the film. Turner's painting of HMS Victory hangs on M's wall behind him. Bond himself is no longer that *"ignominious warship hauled away for scrap."* He now stands in glory atop Whitehall, a hero with his status elevated, marking his identity and fiftieth year in film history. When heroes are on their journey back from adventure, they will have the ultimate glory, the *kleos*, once they have arrived, their return is celebrated.

Xenia

"Mink-lined with first-class service"

Scenes of hospitality in the Bond books and films are key scenes, often where our hero meets the villain and a plot is revealed. The ancient Greeks introduced this to Western literature. It is called *xenia,* which in Greek means guest-friendship. The English word xenophobia, a fear or hatred of strangers or foreigners, is named after it; the noun *xenos* shows respect to both parties in the hospitality, having the dual meaning of guest and host, as well as stranger or foreigner. Whether *Goldeneye*'s Xenia Onatopp is named after this staple of culture is another matter entirely. To some she may be considered to offer extreme and dangerous hospitality!

By way of example, from the first Bond film, over dinner Doctor No is displaying the classical tradition of hospitality, *xenia,* inviting Bond to a lavish silver service dinner before real danger ensues and our villain's diabolical scheme is revealed. Many scenes of *The Odyssey* rely on such exchanges of this interplay and it became a commonplace of Western literature to progress plot, as in life.

Indeed, *xenia* is considered the most important value at the core of *The Odyssey* and introduced the idea to Western literature and a cultured social custom. There is an expectation for visitors that their host provides them with food, bath, friendship gifts, safety for the night, safe escorted travel to their next destination. Odysseus is constantly given drinks on his journeys from seas to shores much like Bond is plied with drinks throughout his adventures.

Homer and other poets used *xenia* to allow the reader to draw the distinction between a good host and a bad host, the hero and the villain. Doctor No of course does not provide a fully hospitable service and therefore, like the Cyclops in *The Odyssey,* should be considered a bad host, in addition to what he has already done and will do to Bond. He has already failed to kill him on multiple occasions to prevent him from investigating him any further; from attempted assassination outside his hotel, poisoning his bottle of vodka, the trespassing tarantula to funeral hearse chase to femme fatale Miss Taro and another assassination attempt by Professor Dent, machine guns, armed guards with dogs, fire-breathing dragon powered by diesel engine, it is remarkable that Bond even reached Crab Key and into Doctor No's lair.

While clearly not in Bond's case here, guests in return for customary hospitality would be expected to pose no threat to the life or property of their host and to return the favour in the future. This underlies nearly every section of *The Odyssey* - Odysseus' encounter with the Cyclops, his stay with the Phaecians to the defeat of the suitors in his own kingdom.

This trope, this *topos,* this commonplace in literature and film allows for such scenes to play out, and plot and character detail to be revealed. As we can see throughout the series, this is now a key expectation for the reader or audience whenever Bond meets the villain.

Xenia plays a key role in establishing relationships in *From Russia with Love*, with coffee medium sweet with Kerim Bay or sussing out Red Grant's red wine with fish on the train. The invitation to Palmyra by Largo in *Thunderball*, to Piz Gloria in *On Her Majesty's Secret Service*, Bond dining with Scaramanga on his island in *The Man With the Golden Gun*, afternoon tea with Hugo Drax in *Moonraker*, dinner at the casino with Kristatos in *For Your Eyes Only*, dinner with Kamal Khan in his palace in *Octopussy*, a guest at Zorin's stud farm outside Paris in *A View to a Kill*, the impact of *xenia* establishing plot, relationships and character for the audience.

"Glad I asked for it shaken."

The modern day films have similar scenes but amongst more action-laden proceedings it is often difficult to pinpoint such moments. Trevelyan dining in his armoured Soviet missile train in *Goldeneye*, Elliot Carver's party scene in *Tomorrow Never Dies,* or Zukovsky offering caviar and sipping vodka with Bond in *The World is Not Enough* are examples of *xenia*, however small the moment may seem. The offer to Jinx of trying Bond's Mojito in *Die Another Day* for instance is not as obvious among the scene-straling Halle Berry and distracting dialogue. Even small moments where he is presented with his famous vodka martini, from *Dr No* through to *No Time to Die*, these small, quiet lifestyle moments of pleasure and pause allow transitions in the plot.

A drink with Severine at the casino in Macau leads to an island meeting with Silva, who is not a good host in *Skyfall*; nor is Blofeld in *Spectre*, meeting Pamola in a Cuban bar, or Bond and Moneypenny visiting Q in his London flat in *No Time to Die*. Like a good meal or a fine wine, these may be small moments but are to be savoured by the audience and allow the story, whether book or film, to breathe.

Life and Death

The mood and overriding tone of death and mortality pervade Fleming's final novel before his own death in 1964, *You Only Live Twice*.

Following the death of his wife Tracy in *On Her Majesty's Secret Service,* a morbid Bond is in a despondent, depressive state in mourning and letting life slide, drinking too much, gambling too much, making him late for work and making mistakes. Later in the novel M says his life was *"going to pieces"*. After psychological profiling from Dr James Moloney, M sends Bond on an *"impossible mission."*

Adding to this theme of death is Dr Shatterhand/ Blofeld's Garden of Death with its poisonous plants, with Japanese men flocking to it to commit suicide, a good death respectable in Japanese culture.

"Die, Blofeld! Die!"

There is a real dark, foreboding, claustrophobic mood to the novel, reflecting Fleming's melancholy at the time. Despite Bond's character being transformed and almost reborn through the story by interactions with his allies Dikko Henderson and Tiger Tanaka and embracing Japanese culture, and exacting revenge on Blofeld, we still leave Bond a shell of his former self. He ends the story with a head injury and left an amnesiac, living the life of a

Japanese fisherman with Kissy Suzuki pregnant with his child, leaving the rest of the world believing he is dead, with his obituary appearing in the newspapers. Fixated on newspaper scraps with reference to Vladivostok, he travels to Russia to discover his true identity.

This was the last Bond novel published in Fleming's lifetime, with his death five months later. Alongside his own declining health, he examines the decline of post-war British power and influence, especially in relation to the USA. This decline was real at the time, with reference to the defection of the Cambridge Spies and the Profumo Affair. The warmth and cooperation of Bond and Leiter in earlier novels is no longer present, replaced by an age of secrecy between the UK and USA in regards to the Asia-Pacific region.

This sense of death and despondency is deliberately emulated in *No Time to Die*, with Bond's death foreshadowed at various moments through the film:

- his disappearance from the gunbarrel with no blood, as he is the one being shot

- the villain Safin meaning 'his death' from the French *'sa fin'*

- *We Have All the Time in the World* ominously playing in the soundtrack, a throwback to Bond's relationship with Tracy ending calamitously in *On Her Majesty's Secret Service,* as well as the OHMSS theme itself when Bond is called back to duty.

- the bells tolling in the square in Matera

- Bond's DNA taken from his toothbrush as well as Madeline's lock of hair

- Blofeld's advice to Bond at Belmarsh saying the truth *"will be the death of you"*

- Bond's infection with Heracles, the name of the viral weapon

- the death of longtime characters Felix Leiter and Ernst Stavro Blofeld

- the revelation that Bond has fathered a child and yet his is a life that forbids the possibility of family, so his life is sure to be short-lived

- the finale on a Japanese Island, just like the novel *You Only Live Twice* where Bond is presumed dead

- M reading an excerpt of Jack London, the same one Fleming used in Bond's obituary in the novel of *You Only Live Twice,* signifying the film's thematic inspiration: *"I shall not waste my days in seeking to prolong them. I shall use my time."*

In this way the accumulation of foreshadowing gives the audience a sense of expectation but also satisfaction, giving some sense of unity to the story by the end on its own terms.

These signs and omens prophesy Bond's fate for the audience to almost expect or be prepared for his death. It was also highly publicised that the film would be the "last chapter" for Daniel Craig's Bond and the twenty-fifth film in the series would "change everything."

In Homer, the gods and heroes speak about destiny like they have full knowledge of the fate they face. Felix being Bond's friend is akin thematically to that of the epic friendship of Patroclus and Achilles. Felix's death foreshadows or at least nods to Bond's own death, as Patroclus' did for Achilles'. In addition, and more imminently, Felix's death spurs Bond into action, to return to MI6, make his services available and take revenge on Ash who killed Felix.

It is worth noting how the different actors playing Bond have portrayed his reaction to death and killing.

In *Dr No* Connery's attitude to the death of Mr Jones is initially one of shock and bemusement while his killing of Professor Dent is cold and brutal. In *From Russia With Love* he has a very subtle sadness to discovering the death of Kerim Bey. In *Goldfinger* he verbalises his wrath to Felix and to M of the deaths of Jill, and then shows remorse for her sister Tilly Masterson. With the deaths of Paula in *Thunderball* and Aki in *You Only Live Twice* these spur Bond into action and not waste any time in progressing his investigation and taking action.

George Lazenby's portrayal, upon the death of Tracy, Bond is wounded personally and shows vulnerablility.

Roger Moore in his films generally shows shock, anger and regret, with one notable exception. In *For Your Eyes Only* he fulfills revenge for Luici and Countess Lisl, and all the other deaths in the film. He shows controlled rage and ruthlessness in kicking Locques' car off the cliff. To a degree he continues this toughness in *Octopussy*.

Timothy Dalton shows remorse and absolute rage and wrath when Saunders is killed. He snaps. Equally so upon the maiming of Felix and the murder of his wife Della. Brosnan shows tenderness when someone he has cared for is killed: Paris, Elektra, even Miranda Frost.

Craig displays rage and regret upon the death of Vesper but also self-recrimination, burying his hurt, unwilling to forgive himself for his stupidity in getting so close to someone, and feels brutally betrayed. He is flippant towards the deaths of Mathis and Severine. He shows true sadness whenever his mother-figure M dies; a coldness, ruthlessness and matter-of-factness to Mr White's suicide. However, he is emotionally intelligent later in the film to protect Madeleine from viewing the recording of her father's death. There is true regret in losing his friend Felix on the ship, while showing cheerfulness in adversity up to the moment he lets him go. He exacts cold revenge on Ash. He is stoic towards his own death, truly accepting of his fate, sacrificing a personal life to that of a spy's, within the world of the film at least.

"I know. I know."

In the ancient world, death was deemed a rite of passage, a transition to the afterlife. People's spirits were considered close to their physical bodies. For the Greeks, the soul left the body, continuing to exist in some form. Socrates in Plato's *Apology* states that once judged the soul would meet the gods and heroes and kings in the Underworld. For the Romans there were no fixed or enforced beliefs. They lived on in the Underworld, an adaptation from Greek culture found in Virgil's *Aeneid*.

What does Bond himself believe of an afterlife? Given the *"Calvinistic atmosphere"* of his schooling, one would suppose he would have had enough grounding in going to chapel to know about sin, an imperfect world, heaven, hell and a perfect Kingdom of God. Bond is a man who loves to live but he is not afraid to die.

Death has been central to the Bond novels and the Eon film series. *No Time to Die* isn't the first time the death of James Bond himself has been considered. During the writing of *From Russia With Love* Fleming had become tired of his creation and ambivalent of his future. He had written to his friend William Plomer that he feared *"staleness"* and *"waring enthusiasm"* for *"this cardboard booby"* so he decided to controversially kill Bond off. However, Fleming seems to have changed his mind, urged by other friends not to kill the golden goose. After working on material for a Bond TV series project which subsequently collapsed, he suddenly realised he had more material for new Bond adventures. Bond in *Dr No* was merely in recovery, in *"convalescence"* from Rosa Klebb's kick in the previous novel.

There seems to be a morbid fascination with death in Fleming's title choices: *Live and Let Die, From a View to Kill, You Only Live Twice*. John Gardner also seems to have realised this: *Nobody Lives For Ever, Death Is Forever, Win, Lose or Die;* Raymond Benson's *The Facts of Death, High Time to Kill.* The films lean into these Flemingesque titles as well when the literary titles dried up: *Licence to Kill, Tomorrow Never Dies, Die Another Day, No Time to Die.*

One of producer Albert R Broccoli's first jobs was working for the Long Island Casket Company, so he got to know all the undertakers and funeral directors of New York City. Even Sean Connery himself worked at one point polishing coffins. Moreover, he finished his last day as James Bond in *Diamonds Are Forever* in a coffin, facing cremation.

We find jokes regarding funerals in *Dr No, Live and Let Die* and *Moonraker.* Bond is an attendee at funerals in *Thunderball, The World is Not Enough* and *Spectre.* He visits graves in *For Your Eyes Only* and *No Time to Die.* There was even a Day of the Dead festival in the opening of *Spectre,* a homage to *Live and Let Die.*

Dicing with death has been a key part of the Bond story. Death should not be surprising for a mortal character such as Bond. He's not a superman. This time, with *no time*, rightly or wrongly, his luck ran out.

Tragedy and Trilogy

Skyfall, Spectre, No Time to Die

Skyfall hints in its final scene that this is the end of the beginning, as M lays on the table a new mission, asking Bond if he is ready to get back to work. However, the film itself is by its nature a new beginning. It starts many years after *Quantum of Solace*, many years after Vesper. There are references to the onset of time, the passage of years. It is the end for Judi Dench's M, the end of an era. In terms of positioning it is more akin to the original twenty films and could nestle on its own terms quite neatly after *Die Another Day*.

In retrospect it was the beginning of the end for Bond himself, in terms of the story for Daniel Craig's Bond at least. *Skyfall* ended up being the beginning of a trilogy, setting up characters and themes for the following two films, culminating in Bond's demise in *No Time to Die*. It seemingly was following the modern cinematic success of Christopher Nolan's *The Dark Knight* trilogy in terms of a clear beginning, middle and end of a character and story arc, while also taking inspiration from Fleming's own loose Spectre trilogy of books from *Thunderball, On Her Majesty's Secret Service and You Only Live Twice*. As a five film unique story arc, perhaps Craig's films could be considered a pentalogy.

To a lesser degree, perhaps some Bond fans can see a very loose trilogy in *Dr No, From Russia with Love* and *Goldfinger* in setting up the character and establishing the series, with each film introducing tropes and creating a formula that arguably used *Goldfinger* as the template for foreseeable entries. Moreover, Connery as Bond is in his prime in these films, and most would agree he is peak Bond in his third film. The film itself is considered the archetype for the films that followed.

One could also consider the first five Connery and Craig films as similar in approach. The first, second, fourth and fifth films of each actor come up against what will be the evil organisation SPECTRE, whereas in their third films, *Goldfinger* and *Skyfall*, each actor comes up against a megalomaniac villain and could simply be standalone adventures with no plot threads between films.

There can also be considered in their tone a trilogy of films by *Goldfinger*'s director Guy Hamilton when he was asked back to direct *Diamonds are Forever, Live and Let Die and The Man with the Golden Gun*. Rightly or wrongly, these films contain a far lighter tone as a reaction to a more serious character-driven piece in *On Her Majesty's Secret Service*, as the franchise attempted to carve a path for the character, with a change in Bond-casting into the 1970s, a very different era from the cool 1960s.

Moreover, the Lewis Gilbert films of *You Only Live Twice, The Spy Who Loved Me* and *Moonraker* clearly share similarities, with their more epic scale, megalomaniac plots to play the superpowers against one another and grand finales of teams of men up against one another to assist Bond in completion of his mission.

The last three Roger Moore Bond films, in *For Your Eyes Only, Octopussy* and *A View to a Kill* directed by John Glen show a more seasoned Bond with younger female companions, similar tone and more focus on action and character, with a harking back to using the Fleming source material. And as Glen continued directing, introducing Timothy Dalton as James Bond with an even more obvious shift to Fleming with a more serious tone and character, fans would long to see what a third Timothy Dalton film would look like. Indeed, one could argue that the tone of *Goldeneye* is very similar to the two Dalton films in terms of character development and personal angle of the plot. The three latter Pierce Brosnan films are certainly more similar in tone with their own style and identity fitting more comfortably with Brosnan's interpretation of the character than in his debut.

Furthermore, Eon make three-picture contracts with their Bond actors to begin their tenures. We can see through the history of the films that for those actors who have achieved over three films, it is their third that is considered their peak performance once they have settled into the role. Beyond the world of cinema, we can see this on television: the third season of a show often is considered the best before the law of diminishing returns, where the plot lines get too convoluted or of lesser quality than before. Maybe three is the magic number.

Trilogies were a hallmark of the first Western tragedian, playwright Aeschylus in the fifth century BC, who contributed much to the development of how we view drama today. He wrote connected tragedies in which each play serves as a chapter in a continuous dramatic narrative. *The Oresteia* is our only existing example of this type but there is evidence that Aeschylus often wrote such trilogies: *Seven Against Thebes, The Suppliants* and *Prometheus Bound* were each a part of his trilogies. Scholars have also suggested several completely lost tragedies based on known play titles. One collectively was called *Achilleis,* comprising *Myrmidons, Nereids* and *Phrygians.* In another he wrote about Odysseus' return to Ithaca after the Trojan War, including the killing of his wife's suitors and its conscquences: *The Soul-raisers, Penelope* and *The Bone-gatherers.*

Tragedies reimagined myths of the Homeric epics that were already identifiable by contemporary audiences. However, their expectations were subverted. The playwrights would put their own spin on these famous myths to say something about contemporary life and politics of the day. Likewise, the Bond films stay contemporary and we know the character of Bond and we have certain expectations of the character. From *Casino Royale* onwards with the character's reintroduction, but more profoundly from *Skyfall* to *No Time to Die*, these expectations are indeed subverted, much like Greek tragedy would do to its audiences of the time. With the Bond producers seeking out greater actors, crew and auteur directors, which demand blockbuster budgets, these trilogy of films were truly of epic proportions and drawing on the epic tradition that the tragedians themselves had done.

Moreover, in literature today, the fantasy *Gormenghast* novels by Mervyn Peake, Robert Harris' Cicero Trilogy of *Imperium, Lustrum* and *Dictator* would fit this mould of Greek tragedy; Stieg Larsson's Millennium Trilogy of *The Girl with the Dragon Tattoo, The Girl who Played with Fire* and *The Girl who Kicked the Hornet's Nest* may be a popular example of where a trilogy is envisaged and takes shape in the popular consciousness. In film we often find an original film but is then followed by two ignominious and disappointing sequels. *The Godfather, Bourne* and *Dark Knight* trilogies are welcome examples where this is thankfully not the case.

The Fourth Protocol

There is also an interesting addendum to this discourse regarding the relevance of trilogies and their structure in Greek tragedy and its connection to drama and series or sequels of films today. In Athens at these dramatic festivals of the fifth century BC, each trilogy was followed by a semi-comic satyr-play. *Cyclops* by Euripides is the only complete example that survives today.

These satyr plays, as an addition to the trilogy of plays, would be written by the same tragedian and offer something of light relief for the audience. They would be semi-comic, satirical with sometimes coarse, ridiculous dialogue and gesturing. They would be a kind of burlesque take of a Greek myth with some connection to the preceding trilogy of tragedies. It became somewhat of a literary art form in themselves, with rules for their composition written by Horace in the first century BC in his *Ars Poetica*.

Two thousand years later, this form of play added to the third in a film series with that weight of expectation from the audience upon it; this could explain why the fourth Bond film goes that bit too far in its style, tone and over-the-top content. Perhaps its spiritual roots were from the seeds of drama in fifth century Athens.

Unless a film series is very self-conscious and careful about its direction, there can be a real risk that this can happen. In terms of Bond, with perhaps the exception of *Thunderball* at the height of the 60s' Bond phenomenon, the Bond films have found their sweet spot in their third films but then the fourth film overreaches itself. While still enjoyable and some solid Bond moments, it is clear that *Moonraker* and *Die Another Day* lose their sense of reality and become somewhat bloated and too fantastical by their third acts: Bond in space, an invisible car, riding a CGI tsunami. One could argue that *You Only Live Twice*, Connery's fifth, is where a course correction and a return to the Fleming source material was required to bring Bond back to basics in *On Her Majesty's Secret Service*.

Even *Spectre,* following *Skyfall,* which was the most successful film in the series to date in terms of ticket sales, with Craig's lighter portrayal of the character and overblown stunts over plot, was a film where there was style over substance. It arguably fell short of its own expectations in the third act, attempting to overcome plot-leaks, rewrites and budget, striving to live up to the success of its predecessor. All these fourth films for a Bond actor since their initial success of Connery in the 1960s seem to suffer this symptom. There has had to be some form of reconfiguration or refresh for Bond's next outing - whether with a new actor, new tone and direction or some serious self-reflection.

Man and Myth

"You only live twice: once when you are born and once when you look death in the face."

The use of the demi-god turned god Heracles of Greek myth is an important aspect of the plot of the most recent Bond film. This is no accident. A weaponised virus that Bond himself becomes infected with and will carry with him to the end of the film, Bond is now inextricably linked with Heracles. The full original myth can be found in Sophocles' *Trachiniae* and in Ovid's *Metamorphoses (Book IX)* should you choose to delve deeper.

In *No Time to Die*, Bond's death cements him as an immortal character, just like the Greek heroes, the first heroes in Western literature, who were demi-gods seeking glory and immortality but who only achieved it in death or sacrifice. The significance of Heracles in the plot, the only hero/demi-god who was granted immortality by the Olympian Gods through fulfilling his twelve trials, is all symbolic of this. Is Craig's Bond now sitting on Mount Olympus, a modern day Heracles? This goes way beyond escorting the Queen to the opening ceremony of London 2012 Olympic Games.

M's scheme is entitled Project Heracles because in Greek mythology Nessus was a centaur killed by Heracles. He uses an arrow dipped in the venom of the Lernaean Hydra. But Nessus tricks Heracles' wife Deianara into giving her husband a shirt stained with the poison. This ultimately kills Heracles. This is the weapon's fate. This is Bond's fate. So Heracles is Bond and Bond is Heracles. For those who knew their Greek myth, the ending of the film would have come as little surprise. Or at least not as big a shock.

Like Heracles, Bond's legendary status was therefore fully embraced by the franchise at the end of *No Time to Die*, capping off the Elizabethan age on Her Majesty's Secret Service and looking towards the future with a fresh beginning. Alongside the foreshadowing of Bond's demise in the film itself, it also fortuitously predicted the death of Queen Elizabeth II and a lifetime of service for one's country. Moreover, the longest-serving Bond actors, Sean Connery and Roger Moore - legends themselves - had died before the film's release; perhaps Bond's death in this film was fitting. Nobody lives forever. Not even James Bond.

His mortality is part of what makes him the most interesting of modern heroes, set among a marketplace of Marvel superhero blockbusters. One could say there is now a sense of real jeopardy of the fate of our hero. However, the producers are unlikely to retread this ending. However debatable and controversial, sparking a plethora of fan discussion, it was different. It's now done and dusted.

One could say all this poses a problem for the producers, others an exciting opportunity to introduce a new Bond *in media res*, amidst matters, with no set-up necessary: just a new mission on *His* Majesty's Secret Service, embarking upon a new Carolean era.

So to call out the 'death' of Bond is premature. As a way to round off twenty five films, two generations of film work by Eon Productions so far as well as a way for Daniel Craig to end his tenure, that's that. However, just as there was a conceit at the beginning of his tenure in *Casino Royale* after twenty films, that we were meeting this character of Bond for the very first time, so too is there a conceit in his death, with a reference to Fleming's own writing.

Fleming tricked his readers into Bond's death in his obituary towards the end of *You Only Live Twice*. He writes, through the words of M, that Bond is *"missing, believed killed, while on official mission to Japan."* Yet Bond returns in the book *The Man with the Golden Gun*, ironically published in 1965, posthumously to Fleming's death in 1964. Wasn't Bond in *No Time to Die* on an official mission on a Japanese island, its territory disputed? M in the film even recites the quote used at the end of the obituary in the *You Only Live Twice* novel, *"I shall not waste my days in trying to prolong them. I shall use my time."* So there is a certain intertextuality where two mediums merge; the cinema audience can surely accept this conceit and accept the words *"James Bond Will Return"* as promised at the end of each previous official Bond film.

Admittedly there was a strong expectation at the end of every film for Bond to survive: he is the perennial hero in the public cultural psyche. He is someone you can trust to be out there, somewhere in the world to root out, tackle and conquer evil in the world. Despite the films playing with themes of death throughout the years, there was no precedent for the death of Bond himself. It was therefore such a shock and surprise, however unpleasant and unexpected.

In retrospect, there was foreshadowing of Bond's fate peppered throughout the film: from the gunbarrel sequence with no blood upon the gunfire, and Bond also disappears as the shot is made, the villain is called Safin - *sa fin* means in French *his end* - the use of the phrase and melody *"We Have All the Time in the World"*, Bond's retirement to Jamaica, Bond is infected with Heracles, the musical reference to Barry's *On Her Majesty's Secret Service*, the stretching of the formula with Bond becoming a father and the knowledge that he has a child; the death of Blofeld and Leiter as if signifying the end of an era.

Foreshadowing was a key plot device in ancient literature to signpost to the reader and audience that something is going to happen, whether for good or ill. Homer would use prophecies and portents in his stories, foretelling future events for the characters and their fates. The fate of Bond in this film was not such a surprise. In the context of the story, whether there was time or not, he had to die.

Those disheartened should, however, take heart and stay strong. Like another great staple fictional character, Sherlock Holmes, resurrected after his supposed death at the Reichenbach Falls fighting his nemesis Moriarty, this

British icon will be back in a next celluloid instalment sooner or later. The other media that Bond already exists in, be it continuation novels or other literature such as comics, the collection of films and novels through the years, audiences can deal with the reality that Bond is alive and well, ubiquitous and eternal as a fictional character. It takes more than a flurry of Royal Navy friendly-fire cruise missiles to kill him off. He survived plenty of firepower throughout the film itself and picked himself up again. Doesn't Bond say in *Skyfall* that his hobby is resurrection?

The Fleming estate seems to be assisting indirectly with his cultural resurrection. Kim Sherwood's trilogy of novels, set in the modern day, following the exploits of three 00 agents in pursuit of the missing James Bond 007 builds towards Bond's return to MI6 and active duty. In the second novel, *A Spy Like Me*, '*"I shall use my time" - Ian Fleming, after Jack London*' opens the novel, which echoes M's words at the end of *No Time to Die*. The ending of the novel reveals a return.

Resurrection is the thematic link between *Skyfall and No Time To Die*. However, in this case Bond's *kleos*, his glory, is more like the hero Achilles than Odysseus. He knows that he will not have a *nostos*. Achilles can either die with glory in battle and have a short life; or not participate and live a long yet insignificant life. Achilles says in Book 9 of *The Iliad:*

My nostos is perished but my kleos will be unwilting

This is Bond's fate being infected as he is with Heracles. He has the choice of dying or living a life without love and endangering those he does love. However, the legend, his *kleos*, lives on, his story deserves to be told. And so the film closes: *"Let me tell you about a man, his name was Bond…"*

Moreover, Charlie Higson's *On His Majesty's Secret Service* was quickly written in time to mark the coronation of King Charles III, resurrecting the character and positing him in this new Carolean era. In an article for *The Guardian* upon the release of the paperback edition, Higson wrote:

"Bond and the royal family are inextricably linked. And Bond is as much a symbol as Queen Elizabeth was. The coronation of King Charles marked a big change. I wanted to investigate that in my book.
"So how to reflect that? To make Bond new, but remain true to the spirit of Fleming? … My 2023 incarnation would have been shaped by a different world in which many of the old certainties of identity, empire, masculinity and nationalism had shifted."

Whether literary or cinematic Bond, the audience, which has throughout the series been deemed relatively intelligent by the Bond producers, can surely equally embrace these propositions and accept another incarnation. It has done so with each recasting of Bond actors before. If there is to be debate and discussion on the future direction of the Bond franchise, then perhaps presence and absence are better words than dead or alive.

• PART II •
MISCELLANEOUS MUSINGS ON THE CLASSICAL CONNECTIONS IN BOND

Dr. No

It may be the first James Bond film but is in fact the sixth Bond literary adventure. Having introduced the spy and the template of the character in *Casino Royale*, an adventure story of treasure-hunting in *Live and Let Die*, a homegrown story in *Moonraker,* an America-bound Bond in *Diamonds are Forever* and an espionage-fuelled Cold War thriller in *From Russia with Love*, with *Dr No* we find a more fantastic story than the previous five novels.

In 1963, Fleming himself acknowledged his plots were *"fantastical while often being based on truth. They go wildly beyond the probable but not, I think, beyond the possible."* Maybe that is the reason that in this novel, one can see the infusion of some literary tropes, with some classical comparisons: the classic 'Theseus and the Minotaur' type of plotting, with Bond discovering Dr. No's lair on Crab Key, Honeychile Ryder's introduction like Venus emerging from the sea, and the themes of power, friendship and loyalty harking back to themes in Homer's *Iliad*.

In terms of meeting Bond, like Homer's *Iliad*, the story starts *in media res*. Bond is a fully formed agent and we get to know him through his actions and reactions. M is a mentor figure like Nestor is to Achilles, the friendship between Bond and Quarrel avenging Strangways comparable in a way to Achilles and Patroclus, the former with an element of dominance and superiority, his friend a sacrificial lamb. And genuine remorse from the hero. Honeychile Ryder as the damsel requiring rescue, scarred by rape, like Briseis saved from Agammemnon by Achilles. These are literary tropes throughout Western literature, motivators for the plot.

The novel of *Dr. No* has been an introduction to the James Bond character for many readers through the decades. Indeed, it was my first secondhand Pan paperback I bought for a pound. Even Bond continuation author Anthony Horowitz speaks emotionally about being inspired by picking up the film tie-in edition for the first time and was inspired to write fiction himself.

Bond introduces himself to Sylvia Trench and the silver screen, masterfully executed by Sean Connery, but the other eternal image of the film is surely Ursula Andress emerging from the sea as Honey Ryder.

The book is blatant in using the simile of the goddess Venus emerging from the sea:

The whole scene, the empty beach, the green and blue sea, the naked girl with the strands of fair hair, reminded Bond of something. He searched his mind. Yes, she was Botticelli's Venus, seen from behind.

The Roman goddess Venus, the Greek Aphrodite, is the goddess of love, both intellectual and sensual, of beauty, charm and fertility, and is consort to Mars, the war god. According to Hesiod, she sprang from the foam (*aphros*) of the sea, from the severed parts of the god Uranus when castrated by his son Cronos. Yes, Greek myth is full of this kind of detail! In Roman myth, Venus also takes on the role of protector of sailors and is a goddess of war.

When commissioning Pat Marriott to illustrate the cover of the original book, Fleming instructed that Honeychile Ryder be shown on a *Venus elegans* shell like the Botticelli painting. Understandably for the film audience the focus, in the film dialogue at least, is on Honey's shell rather than Fleming's description of her nakedness safe for a knife belt.

"There are no such things as dragons."

Superstition and fear play a strong role in the story of *Dr. No*, the villain's mystique overshadows his island, Crab Key. It all adds to the tension and suspense for the audience.

The mystery and threat of Doctor No permeates the piece, as soon as Bond arrives in Jamaica on his assignment. From Mr Jones biting into cyanide hidden in his cigarette to Professor Dent's lies to the femme fatale Miss Taro. All of them are terrified of this controlling menace. Bond recognises this and vanquishes each obstacle placed in his way: the tarantula in his bed, avoiding assassination by the 'Three Blind Mice', uses his charm against Miss Taro and his cold blood against Dent. Bond plays on their fear.

He is struck by the native superstition of his island ally Quarrel, who believes that there is a dragon on Crab Key. However, Bond is also empathetic that he doesn't want him to do something he is not comfortable doing. Later on Bond solves the mystery that it's a dragon run by diesel engine, cutting through both Quarrel and Honey's naivety.

From Russia With Love

Holding back the hero

Some commentators note that keeping Bond apart from the story until more than a third of the way through the novel is a bold move. It was echoed somewhat in the film when we see the real James Bond only after the title sequence and after key plot points are revealed.

This was a daring literary device by Ian Fleming but it does have some basis in Ancient Greek literature. In Homer's *Odyssey* we don't encounter Odysseus until Book 5. Until that point his exploits are alluded to by other characters, principally his son Telemachus and the goddess Athene.

The *Telemachy* serves as an introduction therefore to *The Odyssey* itself, a sort of pre-title sequence to the main feature.

Telemachus journeys from home for the first time in search of news of his missing father. It is also about Telemachus asserting his authority as he gravitates from boyhood to manhood: in Book 1 he admonishes his mother, Penelope; in Book 2 attempts to stand up to the suitors; in Book 3 he is schooled in the social contract; in Book 4 Menelaus educated him with tales of bravery and cunning to inspire him to take action against the suitors. It abruptly ends with the suitors setting an ambush for Telemachus at a harbour, much like SMERSH/SPECTRE set up an ambush for Bond with the Spector/Lektor decoder respectively.

This plot device of ambush and holding back our hero is emulated in John Gardner's thrilling *Nobody Lives Forever*, with an international coordination of assassins competing to kill James Bond.

Gladiators

The training school on SPECTRE Island was inspired by the 1960 film *Spartacus*. In it a Thracian Spartacus in the first century BC is enslaved and then leads a rebellion against Rome and 70,000 enslaved people in the Third Servile War. The Roman Republic had slid into corruption and menial work was carried out by slaves. Spartacus is so uncooperative in his mining position that he is sentenced to death by starvation. However, a businessman named Lentilus Batiatus is impressed by Spartacus' savagery and purchases him for his gladiatorial school (*ludus*) near Capua. He instructs the trainer Marcellus to not overdo his indoctrination. believing that the slave "has quality."

In *From Russia With Love*, Walter Gottell, who would later play General Gogol, the head of the KGB in the Roger Moore era, here plays Morzeny, SPECTRE henchman who trains the personnel on SPECTRE Island. Does this character name Morzeny directly echo that of the Roman Marcellus?

Ultimately, the idea of gladiatorial combat is of course emulated in *From Russia with Love* in its climactic brutal fight between Red Grant, set up as SPECTRE Island's best recruit, and James Bond on the Orient Express. The two best fighters battle it out to the point of death.

Historical accounts of the Spartacus story come from the biographers Plutarch and Appian writing a century later. Spartacus' revolt was a significant challenge for the Roman Republic and Marcus Licinius Crassus was tasked to suppress it. Spartacus' forces were ultimately defeated in 71 BC. Spartacus was presumed killed in the final battle and the six thousand surviving rebels were crucified along the Appian Way.

Travel

Much like Bond's travels in post-war 1950s and '60s, travel in classical times to exotic locations was considered a special, exclusive pursuit. Apart from social motivations, most travel was difficult and expensive, carried out in the interests of warfare, diplomacy or trade. Escapist as it is, most of ancient literature is therefore concerned with travel. *The Odyssey* is about Odysseus travelling home to Ithaca, *The Aeneid* with Aeneas' flight from Troy. Herodotus travelled across Europe and through into Asia, while Caesar wrote accounts of his various wars. Literature is also concerned about the *mores* of travel.

Maritime travel, passage by ship, was considered considerably more pleasant than by road. There was a risk of pirates and hostage-taking in Greek times but the danger of shipwreck was far more a concern for the Romans. The road system in fifth century BC was difficult and time-consuming, whether on foot or on horseback. Greek roads were poorly developed and at risk of highwaymen, whereas Roman roads were extensive but poorly maintained.

Bond travels in luxury and the Orient Express westwards in *From Russia with Love* is just that. Whereas the first Bond film was firmly set just in Jamaica once off the plane from London, in the second film travel and transport is more of a theme. Bond enters Istanbul by plane and then escapes westwards having stolen the Lektor decoder - car, train and speedboat. Travel leads to adventure, and danger, for Bond just like the literature of old.

Goldfinger

The Man with the Midas touch whom Auric Goldfinger shares a love of gold is the legendary king of Phrygia. After being hospitable and generous to the satyr Silenus, companion of the god Dionysus, Midas is granted a wish. He wished all that he touched would turn to gold.

However, when he realised this applied to his food as well, he revoked the gift. He was advised to wash in the river Pactolus. Ever since it has had sands containing gold. It is also told in myth that Midas captured Silenus in his garden to learn of his wisdom. He made him drunk with wine and according to one version of the myth, Silenus said that it was best for a man not to be born at all, or once born to die as soon as possible.

There is also the account of Midas judging a musical contest between Apollo and Pan, he judged unwisely against Apollo. The god then in return gave him ass' ears to show his stupidity, something which Midas did his best to hide, whispering the news into a hole in the ground and filling it up. However, reeds grew over the hole and repeated the story while the wind blew.

So like Goldfinger, Midas is a poor judge and must face the consequences of his actions, playing his golden harp so to speak.

A BOND ODYSSEY

"Shall we make it a shilling a hole?"

Apart from Bond playing cards at the casino table in *Dr. No*, *Goldfinger* is the first film where sport plays an important role in revealing character, principally that of Goldfinger himself - first his cheating at canasta, then on the golf course.

Sport has early links with warfare and entertainment. It teaches us lessons about social change, human skill, military training, with competition used as a means to determine individual fitness for service. The Ancient Egyptians developed the sports of wrestling, weightlifting, rowing, archery, fishing, athletics, ball games among others. In Ancient Greece, in Crete there was bull-leaping and bullfighting. The origins of Greek sporting festivals may date to funeral games of the Mycenaean period, from 1600 BC to 1100 BC. In *The Iliad* there is a description of funeral games for deceased warriors, those held for Patroclus by Achilles. In this period sport was the occupation of the noble and wealthy. In *The Odyssey*, Odysseus proves his Royal status to King Alcinous by showing his proficiency to throw his javelin. Later in 776 BC the Olympic Games were founded which took place every four years, an Olympiad, until 393 AD.

The traditional team sports are seen as primarily springing from Britain, exported across the British Empire: cricket, football sports, bowling, snooker and tennis. Professionalism became prevalent and with the increasing values placed on those who won, so too came the increased desire to cheat. The rising influence of the upper class also produced an emphasis on the amateur and the spirit of "fair play", alongside that of "social discipline" and "loyalty", aspects of empire etiquette which bled into sporting etiquette. These are the roots of the sophisticated settings and atmosphere in which Fleming lets Bond do battle.

The literary Bond is famous for his battles with the villain in an elegant sporting setting. One thinks of the famous bridge scene in *Moonraker* against Sir Hugo Drax. Sebastian Faulks pits Bond against the villain in a tennis match in the Fleming centenary novel *Devil May Care*. The Bond of the films, among scenes at casinos, plays golf against Goldfinger, clay pigeon shooting with Largo, and fencing against Gustav Graves.

Au (from the Latin *aurum*) is of course the chemical symbol for gold, hence the name Auric.

While in passing, the trick wheel tyre-cutters on the Aston Martin DB5 is a throwback to Roman chariot-racing, especially as depicted in 1959's film adaptation of *Ben Hur*.

Thunderball

The name of Largo's vessel, *Disco Volante,* means *Flying Saucer.* It is an Italian name but has its roots in the Latin word, *volo, volare:* to fly. Largo's yacht in the rogue remake of *Thunderball, Never Say Never Again,* merely translates the Italian into English for her name.

The ancient Greeks named their ships since the story of Jason's quest for the Golden Fleece. Jason gathered heroes from all around Greece for this mission, using a ship called *Argo* ('Swift', a male name) in honour of its owner Argos. The heroes who sailed in it were therefore the Argonauts (*Argonautai*).

Unless a ship was somehow special, a poet would not burden his reader or audience with names of heroes' ships. Homer's epic catalogue of ships in Book 2 of *The Iliad* may be the notable exception. *Salaminia* and *Paralos* in Aristophanes' *The Birds* were both sacred ships used as messenger ships or to transport special to delegations. Attic inscriptions from the fourth century BC - *Tabulae Curatorum Navalium* - listed names of ships, all female, derived from heroines and goddesses, places, objects, concepts, descriptions and verbs. There are around three hundred listed. The Egyptians and Romans named their ships in a similar fashion. e.g. *Pandora, Hellas, Sling, Justice, Freedom, Swift, Cupido, Hercules.*

The *Disco Volante* plays a major role in the plot of *Thunderball* as a means of hijacking and camouflaging the RAF Vulcan Bomber and appropriating its two atomic bombs, holding the West to ransom. Bond is invited to Palmyra, Largo's home and to a tour of the ship. Later, holding one of the bombs, Largo uses the ship to escape the climactic battle between Western and SPECTRE agents, with Bond boarding by stealth and Domino taking revenge on Largo for holding her captive.

Largo's sinister relationship with Domino is almost akin to Agamemnon's relationship to Briseis, where a wrathful Achilles must come to her rescue as does Bond. His sinister eye patch, one-eyed like the monstrous Cyclops, with his father Poseidon, god of the sea, who is the obstacle to Odysseus on his journey home.

The climax of the film being an epic seafight between Western agents and SPECTRE is visually striking, with its contrast of red and black scuba suits, harpoon spearguns in hand. An equivalent image from ancient literature may be the catalogue of ships enlisted by Menelaus from all the Greek city-states to fight together at Troy. Moreover, it was promised at the beginning of the film that this mission was big, with all the 00s in Europe recalled, in opposition to the SPECTRE meeting scene earlier in the film. There was bound to be an epic battle by the climax, reflecting too the scale of the films escalating over the first four films.

Ancient sea-battles, *naumachiae,* were equally epic. The Battle of Salamis in 480BC was arguably the largest naval battle of the ancient world. The turning point of the Greco-Persian War, the famous Greek naval general Themistocles commanded the Greeks to ultimately conquer the Persian fleet. The Persians suffered a major blow to their prestige and put the Greek allies in a stronger position for their counter-offensive and the balance of power. The battle has gained a legendary status, the events surrounding the event famously adapted for screen in the two *300* films.

You Only Live Twice

After studying for the Bar in late summer of 2007, I followed in Ian Fleming's footsteps visiting both Hong Kong and Japan. In my estimation, Hong Kong had an amazingly cosmopolitan vibe whereas Tokyo felt so different to anywhere I had visited before or since. It is an interesting paradox of a place. They embrace both the past and cherish their ancient traditions but also the future with its most modern technology.

Fleming in his non-fiction work *Thrilling Cities* found Hong Kong exotic but did not seem to appreciate the ambience of Tokyo. Travelling there in the late 1950s and within memory of the Second World War, he may have taken a dim view of the behaviour of the Japanese in both world wars. Like me on the first time I visited the city, he may have found it all entirely foreign, unfamiliar. He therefore may have found the whole experience uncomfortable. His novel *You Only Live Twice* written in 1963 has an air of morbidity to it, reflecting his health at the time, the tragic aftermath for the Bond character of his previous book *On Her Majesty's Secret Service* but perhaps also his attitude to Japan generally. What is fascinating and what shines through compared to the other novels is the travelogue aspect to the story which the plot is built around.

The film also embraces this travelogue approach, with the film almost exclusively set in Japan, showing off a distant land to a worldwide audience. For audiences both in 1967, and since, it is an exotic and rare travel experience. Even heading to the Far East until relatively recently was considered a big deal for most people given the distance it is to travel.

"There is nothing here but volcanoes."

The Japanese have their own ancient traditions free from ancient Greek and Roman influence so it is challenging to find direct comparisons. However, there is an important feature of Japanese life as in the Mediterranean in classical times. When the filmmakers attempted to find a castle like the one Fleming described for the villain Dr Shatterhand/Blofeld in his novel they were disappointed. Japan did not have such castles by the sea. However, they were impressed by the volcanoes.

The conceit of the film's plot is that SPECTRE could actually hollow out a whole volcano crater and install a rocket base and operation without anyone in the world noticing is a feat in itself. For the filmmakers to expect their audiences to accept this fantasy and suspend disbelief is equally amazing if you stop to think about it. But we don't think about it; it is sheer unadulterated escapist entertainment. We go along for the ride.

The following are some significant real volcanoes, their myths, history and their eruptions in classical times.

Thera

The Minoan eruption was a catastrophe that devastated the Aegean island of Thera (modern day Santorini) in c.1600 BC. It destroyed the Minoan settlement Akrotiri. It ravaged communities and agricultural areas on nearby islands as well as the coast of Crete. There were subsequent earthquakes and paletsunamis. It was the largest volcanic event in human history. It erupted numerous times over several hundred thousand years before the Minoan eruption.

In terms of myth, it may have inspired the myths of the Titanomachy in Hesiod's *Theogony*, with elements of Anatolian folk memory as the tale spread west. Hesiod's lines have been compared with volcanic activity: Zeus' thunderbolts as volcanic lightning, boiling earth the sea as a breach of the magma chamber, immense flame and heat as evidence of phreatic explosions, among other descriptions.

Spyridon Marinatos, the man who discovered the Akrotiri archaeological site, suggested that the Minoan eruption is reflected in Plato's story of Atlantis. This idea is prevalent in popular culture but not backed up by current scholarship.

Mount Etna

Enceladus was a giant and one of Zeus' brothers. He built the highest mountain aiming to get to Olympus and take his brother's place. In punishment, Zeus cast a lightning bolt through his construction, collapsing it. The debris buried the giant. Remaining imprisoned, only Enceladus' fuming breath ascended. We call this lava, and this symbolises justification or meaning behind eruptions and earthquakes.

Myths surrounding Aitna, Hephaestus/Vulcan, Aci and Galatea also contain aetiology of Etna. However, the story of Odysseus and the Cyclops Polyphemus is probably the most famous. Odysseus and his men land on Sicily and discover and hide in the Cyclops' cave, taking his wine and cheese. An angry Polyphemus finds them on his return from shepherding his sheep, whereupon Odysseus reveals himself as *mē tis - "Noone"*. This is cunning on Odysseus' part, as one of his nicknames, his epithets, is *metis - "wise/crafty one"*.

When the cannibalistic cyclops Polyphemus threatens to eat his men and save Odysseus for last, a drunk Polyphemus falls asleep and Odysseus and his men hide under a ram. They blind Polyphemus' one eye with a flaming log from the fire. Polyphemus runs from the cave calling upon other Cyclopes that "noone has blinded him" so the other Cyclopes take no notice!

The Cyclops Polyphemus tries to throw wayward rocks at Odysseus' ship as he and his companions escape. His rocks now define the coastline of Aci Trezza, a fishing village near Catania.

Mount Vesuvius

The name Vesuvius derives from the Greek for "hurling violence" and "not quenchable", the mountain sits at the Gulf of Naples in Campania, Italy, which is devoted to Hercules.

The Phlegraean Plain was described as "fiery", from the mountain "spirited forth a huge fire…", it was inhabited by giant bandits, "the sons of the Earth." Hercules pacifies the region and continues with his labours. Herculaneum may be named after him. Both Venus and Hercules were worshipped in the region, the poet Martial relates in 88AD. The region was devastated by the mountain's eruption in 79AD.

On Her Majesty's Secret Service

The immediate and sudden assassination of Bond's new bride Tracy by Ernst Stavro Blofeld and partner Irma Bunt tragically ends this great story by Fleming, closely adapted by the film. It shows Bond distraught at the loss of his wife and the realisation that, living the life of a spy, he cannot have love or endanger those he does love. Echoing the first novel, *Casino Royale,* and his love for Vesper Lynd ripped away from him, this second tragedy indicates Fleming may have intended more character development for his hero than initially thought.

Marriage and marital imagery, brides-to-be meeting untimely deaths, "Brides of Hades", and men laid low by ruinous marriages is an Ancient Greek trope as much as death itself, especially for young women. This is particularly evident in Aeschylus' *Oresteia* in the tragedy *Agamemnon.*

There are peculiarities of Ancient Greek marital and funeral traditions which have a great deal of similarity. Richard Seaford in *The Tragic Wedding* states that in "both wedding and funeral the girl is washed, anointed and given special *peploi* [gowns] and a special *stephanos* [crown] in order to be conveyed on an irreversible, torchlit journey (on a cart) accompanied by song, and to be abandoned by her kin to an unknown dwelling, an alien bed, and the physical control…of an unknown male."

Another Greek word, *proteleia* - sacrifice, indicates the role of woman in these tragedies. To an extent, Tracy is a sacrifice for Bond to continue the life of a spy, however difficult it is for the character of Bond to bear.

No Time to Die, with its echoes and homages of *On Her Majesty's Secret Service,* reverses the ending. Bond himself dies. Bond's realisation that he cannot endanger those he loves or live a life of love. It makes him choose death itself rather than being made for him. For him, his sacrifice allows Madeline and Mathilde to live. This timeline, this iteration of the character, ends.

Diamonds are Forever

In 1954 Fleming read a story in *The Sunday Times* about diamond smuggling in Sierra Leone. Considering this worthy of a potential plot for a novel, he met Sir Percy Sillitoe, ex-head of MI5 who was working for the diamond traders De Beers in a security capacity. The material Fleming amassed from this meeting was used for both *Diamonds are Forever* and his non-fiction work *The Diamond Smugglers*.

The title was based on the famous slogan of De Beers, 'A Diamond is Forever', created by Frances Gerety in 1947 and named 'Slogan of the Century' in 1999 by *Advertising Age*. Fleming had seen the slogan in the American edition of *Vogue*.

The word 'diamond' comes from the Greek word *adamastos*, which also gives us the word 'adamant'. Ancient Greeks believed diamonds to have mystical protective powers. It is from the Greek word *'adamas'* meaning 'invincible' that the word originates.

In Greek mythology, Adamas and Adamant are used to further the link to diamonds. Cronus castrated his father Uranus with an adamant sickle given to him by his mother Gaia. The same instrument is used by the hero Perseus to decapitate Medusa as she sleeps.

Plato suggested that diamonds were actually living celestial spirits embodied in stones, which only added to their mystique and power. The Greeks themselves believed them to be tears of the gods or spirits from fallen stars.

In Roman mythology, Cupid's arrows were diamond-tipped. It was common practice for Romans to wear them, valuing them above all else, including gold. The Greek myth of diamonds was a powerful grip on the Romans. They regarded the diamond as a charm protection keeping them safe from harm. Even soldiers wore them on the battlefield for this reason. However, to cut a diamond was considered a social taboo. Romans believed it to be like an injury to the gods and the diamond would lose its protective properties.

As today, diamonds mark cherished moments, symbolic love, eternal beauty, strength, resilience, commitment, purity and permanence. For Fleming in the world of his novel, the permanence of the gemstones is in contrast with other aspects of the story - love and life. *"Death is Forever. But so are diamonds."* Raymond Benson says that in the novel diamonds are a metaphor for death, and Bond *"the messenger of death."* Coincidentally, when interviewed while filming *Diamonds are Forever* in Holland, a journalist asked Sean Connery how far you can push violence in film, with a wry knowing smile, he replied, "To death."

Live and Let Die

"For twenty bucks, I'll take you to the Klu Klux Klan cook-out."

One cannot ignore the fact that *Live and Let Die* is considered the blaxploitation Bond film set as it is in New York, Florida and the Caribbean - Jamaica doubling for the fictional island of St Monique. It is a film of its time with the contrast between the ethnicity of Bond and the villain being most prominent, most 'black and white' so to speak. The novel held this contrast too, with Fleming at times leaning into racial stereotypes and colloquial terminology of the time, of its time. Bond had gone up against other ethnicities before: the *'half-Chinese, half-negro'* guards of Doctor No, who himself was half-Chinese and half-German; the Russians, the Japanese. It depends how far you wish to give attention and analyse the sense of the other within the books and films. Bond as a secret agent operating internationally has to go up against someone, whatsoever their identity, ethnicity or nationality.

It is worth noting that the ancient Greeks identified themselves collectively as Hellenes who would come together from individual city states in times of war and other areas of collective interest. Whoever was non-Greek speaking were considered *barbaroi* - 'barbarians' for their supposed *ba ba ba* speech to the Greek ear.

Scholars generally agree that Greek and Roman cultures did not think in terms of race and ethnicity. Apart from language and communication, they may instead have thought more in terms of borders, conquests and alliances. It was the idea of 'us and them', whether not-Greek, not-Roman, not-Athenian or whatever. So there was some sense of identity and personal agency with some geography of thought, whether east or west, as explored earlier. Today people identify in many different ways. With these identity-politics to overcome, surely it is right to have respect, be humble and to seek common ground, with an empathy for difference and seek to understand one another. Films today are leaning into this, with diverse or colour-blindcasting to reflect the globalised culture we live in and interact today.

"You have found yourself."

Tarot cards play an interesting part in the film whose roots date back potentially to ancient times. First known as *tronfi* or *tarrocks* is a pack of playing cards used from at least the mid-15tb century in various parts of Europe to play card games such as Tarocchini. The word *taroch* was used as a synonym for foolishness in the late 15th and early 16th centuries. They originate from Italy and later spread to most of Europe. It evolved into a family of games: German *Grosstarok*, French *Tarot* and Austrian *Konigrufen*.

It was in the 18th Century that French occultists made elaborate but unsubstantiated claims about their history and meaning. It led to the emergence of custom decks for use in divination through tarot card reading and cartomancy (fortune-telling). There are therefore two different types of pack in circulation: one for card games and one for divination. There are four suits variable by region, with the "Fool" acting as a top trump or to avoid following suit.

The early French occultists claimed that tarot cards had esoteric links to ancient Egypt, Kabbalah and India Tantra, but scholarly research does demonstrate their northern Italy 15th century heritage, in Ferrara and Milan.

Historians have described western views of the Tarot pack as *"the subject of the most successful propaganda campaign ever launched… an entire fake history and false interpretation of the Tarot pack was concocted by the occultists and it is all but universally believed."*

The Man with the Golden Gun

Duels and Duelling

Perhaps the greatest formal duel in the Bond films, and what could be considered the highlight of the film in many respects is that between Bond and Francisco Scaramanga, the eponymous man with the golden gun of the title. In both the book and the film the stories build to this moment. The two men are both assassins, but whereas Scaramanga ruthlessly kills for money, Bond does so for Queen and Country, and takes no pleasure in doing so. These are the opposition lines that mark the duel to decide upon who is the best of the two men.

In ancient literature duels were an important aspect where characters prove their code of honour. One thinks of Achilles and Hector in *The Iliad*, Aeneas and Turnus in *The Aeneid*. Armies would typically line up and various champions take each other on in individual combat.

The duel between Penthesilia and Achilles is particularly lauded on a lot of vase paintings. Penthesilia was the daughter of Ares (god of war) and Otrene (Queen of the Amazons). She first fights Ajax but this ends in a draw, whereupon Achilles enters the fray and duels her, striking her in the chest and she falls.

The classical Greeks were very keen on the Homeric combats generally: Hercules and Atreus, Menelaus and Paris were notable too. Even in later literature we find the duel playing an exciting role in climaxes to plots: *The Three Musketeers, The Count of Monte Cristo* by Alexandre Dumas and *Cyrano de Bergerac* by Edmond Rostand. In modern times we find Horatio Hornblower *"demand satisfaction"* to reclaim his honour against Jack Simpson in *Mr Midshipman Hornblower* by CS Forrester. And in cinema we see not only James Bond don traditional fencing attire for gentlemanly dueling against Gustav Graves at Blades in *Die Another Day,* but also Harry Potter sparring against Voldemort with wands and John Wick in multiple duels with guns and martial arts in their own series of films.

The Spy Who Loved Me

The villain Karl Stromberg's aquatic lair, along with his vision for a subaquatic future, Atlantis has its origins in a fictional island in Plato's writings *Timaeus* and *Critias*. It is part of an allegory of the hubris of nations.

The legend of Atlantis is a story about a moral spiritual people who lived in a highly advanced, utopian civilisation. However, they become greedy, petty and morally bankrupt. The gods became angry because the people had lost their way and turned to immoral pursuits. This story is befitting of Stromberg, as it is the decadence of Western and Eastern powers of the Cold War that he delusionally feels so strongly and to whom feels morally superior.

In the story of Atlantis, it is described as a naval empire that ruled all parts of the known world. However, after an unsuccessful attempt to conquer 'Ancient Athens', it falls out of favour with the gods and submerges into the Atlantic Ocean.

The story has had considerable impact on literature, regarded as utopian by Renaissance writers such as Francis Bacon and Thomas More. It has become a byword for all the prehistoric lost civilisations and continues to inspire contemporary fiction. *The Spy Who Loved Me* is just one example.

Plato may have been inspired himself from Egyptian records of the eruption of Thera in 1628BC, the Sea Peoples invasion or the Trojan War. Others suggest Plato just created the account himself, with loose inspiration from contemporary events such as the failed Athenian invasion of Sicily in 415-413BC or the destruction of Helike in 373BC.

In *Timaeus,* Socrates muses about the perfect society described in Plato's *Republic. In Critias,* ancient Athens seems to represent the "perfect society", Atlantis its opponent, its antithesis of the perfect traits described in the *Republic.*

Moonraker

While *The Spy Who Loved Me* had a megalomaniac villain seeking a world completely underwater, *Moonraker* develops this idea but transplanting it to space. Through a concentrated and manipulated chemical extract from *Orchidae Nigra,* a Black Orchid, into the nerve gas X-52, the master plan is the destruction of every human being in the world and to repopulate Earth with a master race of superior, ideal, supermodel specimen humans, like a modern day Noah Ark story.

The Biblical parallels are clear. As Bond and CIA counterpart Holly Goodhead approach the space station in a stolen Moonraker shuttle, they take note of the cargo: several pairs of couples; a reference to Noah's Ark in Genesis.

In Genesis, God tells Abraham that he is going to destroy men because of their wickedness, for turning away from Him *en masse*. Noah and his family alone are to be favoured and spared among all humans. God instructs Noah to construct a large vessel to store examples of every land animal in creation. Hugo Drax in the film represents both God and Noah. However, there is no justification whatsoever for Drax's actions. They are testament to genocide, and Drax is more akin to the Nazi roots of the character in Fleming's original novel.

For Your Eyes Only

"ATAC to St. Cyril's, ATAC to St. Cyril's"

St Cyril's is an abandoned Eastern Orthodox monastery in Greece situated at the top of a rocky outcrop 400m high.

Filmed at the Holy Trinity Monastery (*Agia Triada*) iin Central Greece, it is situated in the Peneas Valley north east of the town of Kalantaka. It forms part of twenty four monasteries originally at Meteora on the oldest still existing of the Meteora monasteries. Meteora means *"suspended in air."* It was constructed in the fourteenth and fifteenth centuries and is included in the UNESCO list of World Heritage Sites.

St Cyril himself, born c.313 AD and died in 386 AD, is best known for his defence of the doctrine of the Incarnation (that the one person of Jesus was the divine Son, the second person of the Trinity) and for his exegetical writings. He was well-read in both the Christian theologians and Greek philosophers. He was a deacon, priest, preacher and liturgist and generally an important figure in Christianity still today.

Ships and other vessels

For Your Eyes Only has numerous vessels with names of classical resonance:

The Triana - in reality *Botje & Ensing Zurga*. The name comes from the Roman emperor Trajan, meaning "three rivers". It also has a Greek origin from the names Katrina or Katriana meaning "clean" or "pure". Perhaps this name is significant given the murders of the Havelocks, Melina's parents, at the beginning of the film. They are innocent, clean of any wrongdoing.

Neptune - named after the Roman god of the sea, the Greek name being Poseidon.

Mantis - although now more associated with the insect, *mantis* is the Greek word for a diviner, a "prophet" or "seer". The first known *mantis* in Greek literature is Calchas, the army's official *mantis* in the first scenes of the *Iliad*.

Panther - this is in fact a Greek word for the same creature.

St Georges - the trawler disguising what is really a British spy ship. It hits and is destroyed by a World War 2 mine at the start of the film. It contains the secret ATAC system which becomes the MacGuffin for the plot. Each side - the British, the Soviets with Kristatos - is hurrying to appropriate this to gain an upper hand in Cold War politics.

SS Columbina - Columbo's boat

Octopussy

Octopi in literature are deemed to evoke fear and terror but can also symbolise hidden truths or the obscure. The former meaning would explain why the symbol of the organisation SPECTRE in the Bond series is an octopus, but in both the *Octopussy* short story and the film, it is arguably the latter.

In the short story Bond tracks down Major Dexter Smythe for him to reveal the truth of hidden Nazi gold. By the end of the story, Smythe is hunting for scorpion-fish to feed his pet Octopussy but suffers a sting and is dragged underwater by Octopussy as the poison sets in. Bond views the death as suicide but puts it down as unofficial drowning. In the film, it is Octopussy and her all- female cult organisation that is hiding a smuggling operation. The story of her hidden background is also revealed to Bond as daughter of Smythe, as a nice nod to the original short story by Fleming.

Octopuses appear in mythology as sea monsters like the Kraken of Norway and the Akkorokamui of the Ainu and the Gorgon of ancient Greece. In more modern times, a battle with an Octopus appears in Victor Hugo's book *Toilers of the Sea* as well as inspiring Fleming.

Symbolically they represent qualities of versatility, agility, intelligence, awareness - much like Octopussy's female followers in the film - as well as regeneration and infinity. Like Bond and Odysseus, the octopus is considered the king of disguise, full of ploys to pass unnoticed by his predators.

The octopus has had a huge impact on the art and mythology of Minoan/Cretan and Greek culture. It is considered a prototype for the multi-headed Hydra and Medusa. In the eyes of the ancient Greeks, the octopus and Odysseus were both known as *polymetis* - of much wisdom and cunning. Through disguise and deception the octopus can outwit predators by taking on the same colour as whatever surface he clings to and turn the world black with his ink and render itself invisible. Fishermen would only be able to lure the male octopi out with female octopi, their fatal weakness. Likewise with this exception, through his own wit and cunning, Odysseus was able to outwit monsters and win, psychologically and physically, much like Bond himself.

Island Paradise

The idea of an island populated exclusively by women would certainly have been a challenge. Arousing Bond's curiosity and interest, this sort of island, Octopussy's floating palace, has links to those in ancient literature.

One scene in *The Odyssey, in Book 6* springs to mind: when Odysseus arrives shipwrecked on the island of Scheria, ruled by the Phaecians. The morning after his landing, Athene, disguised as a friend of King Alcinous and Queen Arete, sends their daughter Nausicaa and some of her handmaidens to wash clothes near the spot where Odysseus has collapsed. Nausicaa seems immediately attracted to Odysseus. She tells him how to find the king and queen and how to endear himself to them and ensure a safe voyage home. He is subsequently received well and he reveals his identity. He welcomes their offer to return home to Ithaca.

This Phaecian section of *The Odyssey* seems most likely influenced by folk tales. It is a genre found in many cultures, where a beautiful innocent young woman, often a princess, is attracted by a rugged handsome stranger who usually is older and always more experienced. They may end up together; more often the man makes an impression and then moves on. This is a popular theme in drama, as the film *Octopussy* with the relationship between Bond and Octopussy attests.

In the case of Odysseus, he acknowledges the charms of the virgin Nausicaa but is intent on returning to Penelope. There is no room to hang about and have a dalliance. In Bond's case, he has no intention of being an imprisoned guest of Octopussy in the palace as the plot thickens, he must follow the trail and complete his mission to save the world. He has his dalliance to gain Octopussy's trust and then escapes.

Phaeacia is a Utopia, just like Octopussy's floating palace. The people there are civilised and polite, with minor exceptions. The Phaeacians go above and beyond for Odysseus, much like Octopussy instructs her followers to show every courtesy to Bond. The island itself is a paradise: luxuriant orchards, featuring an array of different fruits, vegetables and grains aplenty.

The Phaeacians excel at seamanship - much like Octopussy's followers' ins and outs on the rowbarge, dancing and sports - like Octopussy's circus performers.

Appearance and Reality

Athene devotes her talents to the task of making Odysseus - and Telemachus - look impressive: taller, bigger, more splendid. Disguises and dress play a more prominent part in *Octopussy* as well. Bond uses many disguises in the film to fulfill his objectives: a South American colonel, a crocodile, a corpse, a manufacturer's representative from Leeds, a circus knife thrower and a clown.

A View to a Kill

The catalyst of the plot for the fourteenth James Bond film is the *"leading French industrialist"* Max Zorin's use of microchips to improve performance in his horse Pegasus to win at horse racing. He has a sale of horses at his stud farm outside Paris which Bond and his jockey club expert Sir Godfrey Tibbett visit to investigate further. Bond, under the disguise of St John Smythe tries out the spirited horse Inferno while pitted against an array of obstacles on the racing ground by Zorin before his cover is blown.

In ancient Greece horses were given the highest regard by the upper class who could afford these expensive creatures, especially given their significance to the Greek gods. Especially those bred in Thessaly, they were used for hunting, racing and travelling, warfare and trading, depicted on vases and sculptures, esteemed by the elite. Famous horses such as Arion known for its swiftness, Achilles' horses Balius and Xanthos, Hippocampus that pulled Poseidon's chariots and Pegasus, the flying horse sprung from the blood of the Gorgon Medusa proliferated Greek myth. And then, of course, the famous wooden horse, the Trojan Horse, the symbol of Troy.

Alexander the Great's horse Bucephalus, whose name literally means 'ox-headed', is one of the most famous in ancient Greece. Described as an imposing creature with an imposing head, with a thick black coat and a white star on his brow. Alexander alone was able to tame

Bucephalus realising that the horse was afraid of its own shadow. He won this wager to tame the horse from his father.

The Athenian historian Xenophon in *The Art of Horsemanship* wrote about looking after horses, pointing out that the golden rule is to approach horses with care and not to get angry with them. Good advice for anyone invited to horse racing in the future.

The Living Daylights

"Death to spies"

Smiert Spionam - Death to Spies - is a supposed Soviet operation to kill British and American agents reactivated from the time of Stalin and SMERSH under the guise of the KGB in the '80s world of the film. It is in fact a way for General Georgi Koskov to feign defection and to misinform and manipulate British Intelligence and a way to assassinate General Pushkin, head of the KGB, set up an arms and drugs deal in Afghanistan and ultimately take control of the KGB himself. *The Living Daylights* offers the audience a more espionage-fuelled caper than other entries and it does require the viewer to pay attention to various machinations of the plot.

Homer reveals acts of spying in Ancient Greece during the Bronze Age in the 12th Century BC. In the *Iliad* Book 10, Homer describes Odysseus and Diomedes embarking on a reconnaissance mission one night to discover more about the Trojans' plans. That same night a Trojan named Dolon (interestingly his name derives from the Greek word for deceit - *dolos*) promises Hector that he will spy on the Greeks and infiltrate their camp. He is captured by Odysseus and Diomedes uncovers useful intelligence, but ultimately they renege on sparing his life. They cut off his head. This chapter in the Trojan War story is described as "The Doloneia" and is a distinct section of the *Iliad*. In *The Odyssey*, Helen recounts how

Odysseus infiltrated Troy dressed as a house slave, able to glean intelligence for the invading Greeks.

In the fourth century BC Aeneas Tacticus, a renowned military writer, emphasised the significance of what we would today describe as Military Intelligence - knowing one's geography and effective defensive warfare. Areas for intelligence-gathering included ports where merchants, travellers and ambassadors would have valuable information. However, what could be honest advice could in fact be misleading. There was severe punishment, including torture and execution, if spies were caught.

Alexander the Great used espionage and covert agents and bribery to infiltrate and undermine Athens. He asked Persian ambassadors about the lengths of roads in Asia Minor and the Persian king's skills. However, little is said of the spies themselves that he deployed. They extracted strategic-level intelligence and interrogation techniques before launching an invasion. He used local guides and scouts to uncover the geography for logistical purposes.

The charming yet manipulative, deceitful, sociopathic General Koskov is akin to a similar classical figure, Alcibiades, the Athenian general and statesman.

Alcibiades played a major role in the Peloponnesian War (431-404BC) as strategic advisor, military commander and politician. However, he changed his political allegiance several times. In the early 410sBC he advocated an aggressive foreign policy and was a prominent proponent of the Sicilian Expedition. After his political enemies brought charges of sacrilege against him, he fled and defected to Sparta. He served there as a strategic advisor, proposing several major campaigns against Athens. However, he made enemies in Spartan as well and defected to Persia. He served the satrap (like a Persian governor) Tissaphernes until Athenian political allies brought about his recall. The Persian governor was even induced by the Spartans to murder him. He was indeed assassinated by Persian soldiers in 404 BC.

Ancient sources are less than edifying about Alcibiades' character. Plutarch describes him as *"the least scrupulous and most entirely careless of human beings."* Diodorus calls him *"in spirit brilliant and intent upon great enterprises"* while the legal speechwriter Lysias stated that *"he repays with injury the open assistance of any of his friends."* He roused fear up his contemporaries for the sake of the political order, particularly when the Herms were ominously desecrated the night before the Sicilian Expedition.

Androcides said that *"instead of holding that he ought himself to confirm with the laws of the state, he expects you to confirm with his own way of life."* Cornelius Nepos commented that Alcibiades *"surpassed all the Athenians in grandeur and magnificence of living."*

Alcibiades was an unscrupulous man, with selfish motives, despite his great charm and brilliant abilities. Psychologist Anna C Salter concluded that he *"had all the classical features of psychopathy."* His confidence and ambition went far beyond his skills. He was also skilled in oratory, the *"ablest speaker"*, saying whatever his audience needed on any occasion.

Alcibiades also had a feud with his political rival, the populist demagogue Cleon. Which leads us back to Koskov who had a feud with his political rival, General Pushkin, head of the KGB in *The Living Daylights*. Both Alcibiades and Koskov are very similar characters.

General Georgi Koskov has high intellect, military training and is skilled in manipulation. He intends to kill General Pushkin and reap the profits from a mass supply of opium bought from the Afghanistan based Mujahedin after smuggling it to the USA (street value $500 million) while bolstering the Soviet occupation of Afghanistan by using advanced weaponry bought from Brad Whittaker. It is one of the rare examples where a Bond film touches on the world politics of the day.

Moreover, Koskov is a corrupt Soviet general in business for himself, who carefully plays both sides of the Cold War. He plays the part of an anxious pawn but is in reality a mastermind using all means to his own advantage. He fakes his own defection at the beginning of the film using his girlfriend Kara Milovy as a sniper to make it look real, and later uses her to distrust Bond, in the end fortunately unsuccessfully. He also uses Colonel Feyador and his airbase in Afghanistan, in the guise of being on an official state mission for General Pushkin. His ultimate goal, though not made overt in the film, is to take control of the KGB, of which he was a part, following Pushkin's assassination.

There are many ways to describe Koskov worthy of a classical villain: a deceitful, sociopathic, two-faced double-crossing character. His ambiguous nature makes him very comparable with the classical figure of Alcibiades in terms of political trustworthiness. It is no surprise that Koskov was ultimately sent back to Moscow *"in the diplomatic bag."* The way he dies, the likely execution on his return befits the way he lived.

Licence to Kill

With its R -Restricted- rating, '15' here in the UK, principally for its violence, it is indisputable that *Licence to Kill* is the most violent Bond film to date. Some would argue that the violence shown on screen is unnecessary but others would say it adds to the hatred one feels towards the villain Sanchez and the satisfaction when Bond finally exacts vengeance for his friend Felix Leiter.

Revenge is a key theme in Ancient Greek literature. In *The Iliad,* Achilles returns to fight for the Greeks and duels Hector for killing his friend Patroclus. The first word of *The Iliad* is *mēnin,* wrath, justified anger. Achilles swears vengeance on Hector and launches himself back into battle. He kills every Trojan who gets in his way, killing so many that their corpses fill the nearby Scamander River. His vengeance is relentless.

The Greek word for vengeance, revenge, retribution, penalty, punishment and/or torture is *timōria*. It is a form of justice befitting a protagonist. The Greeks believed that if any terrible wrongdoing was made on them, they had the right to return the favour in whatever means they felt just. Individuals would demand revenge if they felt humiliated, offended or betrayed. Nemesis was the goddess of revenge, to punish those guilty of hubris or pride, vanity and arrogance.

In *The Odyssey*, Odysseus is out for revenge on the suitors when he returns from his epic journey back to his homeland:

You dogs! You thought I would never come home from Troy. So you wasted my house, forced the women to sleep with you, and while I was still alive you courted my wife. Without my fear of the gods in high heaven or of any retribution from the world of men. Now the net has been drawn tight on you.

Odysseus' anger and justification for vengeance against those who betrayed him is evident.

The gods also take revenge on Odysseus throughout the story, such as Zeus taking revenge on Odysseus and his men as well as Poseidon taking revenge on Odysseus.

Now clearly film and literature are different mediums with the visual leaving nothing to the imagination compared to reading books. However, it is intriguing to take some examples from the film and compare them to the level of violence contained in *The Odyssey*. You can judge for yourself which you consider the more gruesome and the more avenging.

"Looks like he came to a dead end."

In *Licence to Kill* we see Sanchez whipping his mistress Lupe with the tail of a stingray, the murder of a bride and maiming by shark of a bridegroom on their wedding night.

With Bond beginning his personal vendetta of vengeance we see electrocution of a guard by electric eels, death by shark attack, death by spear-gun (*"Compliments of Sharky"*), death by submachine gun more gratuitous than seen before, explosive and bloody death by pressure tank, death by pulveriser via conveyer belt, death by forklift, and finally petroleum-laden, fiery, vengeful death by lighter. Shocking. Positively shocking.

In the final sections of *The Odyssey*, Odysseus returns to his home, his palace in Ithaca and takes vengeance on the freeloading suitors along with the disloyal maidservants of his wife Penelope. With the help of his son Telemachus, Eumaeus and Philoetius he slaughters no less than one hundred and eight suitors. The lead suitor Antinous receives an arrow through his throat from Odysseus' bow. He is considered the main bad apple. Eurymachus takes an arrow in the liver. Amphinomous is speared by Telemachus.

With the doors of the palace locked, valleys of spears are hurled, Odysseus and men kill several suitors while receiving only superficial wounds themselves. Odysseus spares none of them. *"Here is a clear end to the contest. Now I'll see if I can hit another target no man has yet and may Apollo grant my prayer."*

Odysseus has the maidservant Eurycleia come out to round up the disloyal maidservants, clear up the corpses from the hall and wash the blood from the furniture.

• A BOND ODYSSEY •

They are then sent outside and executed. Odysseus tells Telemachus to cut them down with a sword but Telemachus decides to hang them instead - a more disgraceful death. Last of all, the traitor Melanthius is killed. After this bloodshed, Odysseus has the house fumigated to fully clean his house of the suitors.

Goldeneye

"Janus, the two-faced Roman god come to life"

The Roman god of beginnings and endings, of openings and closings epitomises the duality of the villain Alec Trevelyan, formerly 006, in *Goldeneye*. The relevance of the name goes beyond the world within the film, however, with much larger significance for the Bond franchise. This was the last film during the lifetime of Bond producer Cubby Broccoli, the man without whom this series of films would not exist. It was the first film produced by his children Michael G Wilson and Barbara Broccoli, who now took the producing reins. Janus is the god of time and transition and in a way fittingly reflects the making of the film itself. Moreover, *Goldeneye* was considered a soft reboot of the Bond films after a six-year hiatus due to legal disputes.

There is a clear difference in tone and cinematography. We have a new Bond, a new M, new world politics in the aftermath of the Cold War. In this way this was a new beginning and closing the door to the first sixteen films in the history of the franchise. Janus played his part.

"I trust you'll stay on-a-top of things"

The yacht Manticore used by Xenia Onatopp and Admiral Chuck Farrel contains a most alluring classical connection. Akin to the Egyptian sphinx, Manticore was a legendary Persian animal with the head of a man, body of a lion and the tail of a dragon or scorpion. It allies itself with evil creatures. Those in the audience recognising this would realise Bond's suspicions beyond his initial encounters with Onatopp.

In a direct comparison with Xenia Onatopp herself, the Manticore eats its victims whole. It devours its victim, using its three rows of teeth. It leaves no bones behind.

Interestingly the name *manticore* was mistranscribed from the original Persian. The original Persian word *martya -* 'man' and *xar - 'to eat'* was transliterated to the Greek *androphagon - 'maneater'*. The mistranscribed *mantichorus* was in a faulty copy of Aristotle, through whose works the notion of the manticore spread across Europe. This was clearly not lost on the scriptwriters in respect of staying *"on-a-top of things"*.

Finally, Pierce Brosnan and Sean Bean reunited on screen entering the Ancient Greek mythical world for *Percy Jackson and the Lightning Thief* as the centaur Chiron and the King of the gods Zeus respectively fifteen years after *Goldeneye* in 2010.

Tomorrow Never Dies

The significance of Britain's historic naval sea power, its thalassocracy, is a focal point for *Tomorrow Never Dies* and in antithesis to the Chinese airforce. Whether this bore any truth, it romanticises Britain's role and is a snapshot of world politics at the time of both countries' status. How times have changed. If it were filmed today perhaps relations between the USA and China would be more fitting; Bond and Britain would more likely be a mediator, seeking to prevent World War 3 and allay tensions between West and East. In this way it would be more akin to the plot of *You Only Live Twice*, with Britain mediating between the US and Japan. The role of rivals coming together to fight a greater threat is a powerful plot thread overcoming the politics of the day.

Historically, the eighteenth Bond film arrived during the cultural wave of what was termed '*cool Britannia*' signifying anything British being popular and Britain a great place to live.

The Latin word *Britannia* was applied to the British Isles, Great Britain and the Roman province during the Roman Empire, and by the first century BC replaced *Albion* as the prevalent name for the island of Great Britain. It was itself a Latinisation of the Britonnic word *Pretani* and the Greek *Prettanike* and *Brettaniai*. The Romans referred to the British Isles as *Insulae Britannicae*. Emperor

Claudius visited while Britain was being conquered. He was honoured with the agnomen *Britannicus.*

With her connection with conquest, and wearing her helmet, trident and shield, the goddess Britannia looked similar to Athena/Minerva, goddess of victory. On one frieze she is depicted as bare breasted writhing in agony under the heel of the emperor. On a range of coinage she sits on a globe above the waves, Britain on the edge of the known world.

Leaning into Britain's naval role, *Tomorrow Never Dies* harkens back to the classic Bond film *The Spy Who Loved Me,* Elliot Carver seeking monopoly of the media rather than Stromberg's megalomania for a world underwater.

Britain was certainly a thalassocracy in the 18th and 19th centuries building its empire based on its prowess in warfare, trade and administrative process from the Napoleonic Wars onwards.

The female personification of the British Isles, the Roman goddess Britannia holding a shield and spear, which later became a trident in 1797, and a helmet added in 1825 was resurrected in the Renaissance to symbolise the Royal Navy's victories and British maritime power.

Pierce Brosnan in his second outing as 007 is very much Commander Bond, Royal Navy: in military mode as White Knight at the beginning of the film destroying an arms bazaar and preventing a nuclear accident, and, soon after the title sequence, he gets his briefing at the Ministry of Defence. In the latter half of the film we see him in his Naval uniform as he plans to find the HMS Devonshire. In the climax he and his Chinese counterpart Wai Lin are in stealth military fatigues to complete the mission.

The film is a real crowd-pleaser, full action-laden fun with cinematic Bond at the fore, one man to save the day. There are Odysseus-like, cunning qualities through his interactions. He is a man of tricks and deception, infiltrating and disrupting Carver's printing press with his pioneering multifunction Ericsson *"cellphone"*. He has a fully-tricked out BMW 750 like Odysseus' Wooden Horse. He shows foresight in stealing the jet with its F35 nuclear torpedoes to avoid disaster from British cruise missiles. He is up against a Poseidon-like figure with his headquarters or lair by sea using stealth technology and three-pronged, trident-like sea-drill.

The World Is Not Enough

"The captive falls in love with her captor."

The captivity and ransoming of Elektra King, daughter of oil tycoon Sir Robert King, is the springboard for the plot of the film. It is one of the more dynamic plot devices by the scriptwriters for the Bond series. The subsequent discovery that she may have Stockholm Syndrome or that she herself turned the terrorist and anarchist Renard for her own ends has its roots in ancient literature in the myth of Hades and Persephone.

Also known as Kore in Greek myth, Persephone is the daughter of Zeus and Demeter and is snatched to be queen of the Underworld by Hades while picking flowers in Enna, Sicily. John Milton in *Paradise Lost* recounts it as:

> *that fire field*
> *Of Enna, where Proserpine gathering flours*
> *Her self a fairer Floure by gloomie Did Was gatherd, which cost*
> *Ceres all that pain*
> *To seek her through the World.*

(4.268-72)

Zeus gave in to her lamentations but she could not be fully released from the Underworld because she had eaten some pomegranate seeds. It was arranged that she spends eight or six months of the year on earth and the remainder with Hades. Persephone therefore came to represent the seed corn that must descend to earth so that from seeming death there would be new life. She later came to symbolise death, while Hades and his wife represent the rulers of the dead. A fitting comparison for Renard and Elektra.

The very name of Elektra brings to mind the concept of revenge, but here it is not matricide as Electra and Orestes killed Clytemnestra and her lover Aegisthus but instead patricide. In order to reclaim her mother's bloodline and right to the oil, she planted the bomb with the help of Renard to kill her father. However, Elektra is on the point of insanity at this point when she reveals her plan to Bond, bound to a torture chair.

"There's no point in living if you can't feel alive."

Another interesting point to note about the plot is a link with and reversal of roles from the previous instalment, *On Her Majesty's Secret Service*. Bond is taken in by Elektra's charms as a seemingly winged dove, but manipulatively and calculatingly she ends up being the villain.

In this way she is more like the enchantress Medea who initially helps Jason secure the Golden Fleece before conspiring against him in the boldest way possible when he grows tired of her and instead designs to marry the daughter of the king of Corinth. She was the subject of tragedies by Aeschylus, Sophocles and Euripides, but only that of the latter playwright survives. It is well worth reading, or better watching on stage, not least for considering the issue of what is considered premeditated murder and whether there are circumstances where killing can be justified. In Roman times, Seneca the Younger and Ovid also wrote tragedies about her. She is also more romanticised by Apollonius Rhodius, and by Ovid in his *Heroides* and *Metamorphoses*.

The fact that *The World Is Not Enough*'s Elektra reveals she cut off her own earlobe to make her captivity appear genuine is a subtle link to Blofeld cutting off his earlobes to lay claim to the de Beauchamp bloodline and title in *On Her Majesty's Secret Service*. This point of betrayal would not have been lost on the Bond character. Indeed the director Michael Apted sums it up that Bond falls in love with Tracy who is actually Blofeld. Like the Greek myths being reinterpreted and reimagined by different authors and generations, from the epics of Homer to the Athenian tragedies of the fifth century BC and beyond, so too do the Bond plots. This is in recent times especially the case as almost all the Fleming material has been exhausted.

Die Another Day

"Look at him. You'd think he was some kind of hero."

For a film that is much derided and decried, the twentieth Bond film does contain some real classical gems. It adds more of an intelligent and serious dimension amidst the entertaining romp.

The title of the twentieth Eon official Bond film *Die Another Day* is taken from a stanza in the poem *Day of Battle* by poet and classicist A.E. Housman (1859 - 1936), which was part of his collection of poetry *A Shropshire Lad*, self-published in 1896:

Poem LVI

Day of Battle

'For I hear the bugle blow
To call me where I would not go,
And the guns begin the song,
"Soldier, fly or stay for long."

'Comrade, if to turn to fly
Made a soldier never die,
Fly I would, for who would not?
'Tis sure no pleasure to be shot

'But since the man that runs away
Lives to die another day,
And cowards' funerals, when they come,
Are not wept so well at home,

'Therefore, though the best is bad,
Stand and do the best, my lad;
Stand and fight and see you slain,
And take the bullet in your brain.'

The villain Sir Gustav Graves' superweapon Icarus is a reference to the Greek myth of Icarus. With his waxed wings he disobeys his father Daedalus and flies too close to the sun and falls from the sky and drowns. It is a tale of excessive ambition.

The master craftsman Daedalus was the architect of the labyrinth in Crete. King Minos had imprisoned both Daedalus and Icarus on suspicion that they had revealed the labyrinth's secrets to Theseus by giving Ariadne a ball of string as a clue to find and rescue her from the Minotaur. Icarus and Daedalus escaped using wings that Daedalus constructed from feathers, threads from blankets, clothes and beeswax.

Daedalus had warned Icarus first of complacency and then of hubris, instructing him to fly neither too low nor too high, so the sea's dampness did not clog his wings nor the sun's heat to melt them. The lengthiest account of the myth can be found in Ovid's *Metamorphoses Book VIII lines 183 - 35*. The idiom "fly too close to the sun" derives from the myth, but clearly not taken on board by Gustav Graves; he burns the wings off his own Antonov plane over the Korean peninsula. It is no accident that his alter-ego is Colonel Tan-Sun Moon, a subtle link to the Icarus character flying too close.

Moreover, in psychology the Icarus complex is defined as "a form of overcompensation wherein an individual, due to feeling of inferiority, formulated grandiose aspirations for future achievement despite lacking proper talent, experience, and/or personal connections. Such a person often exhibits elitism fueled by hubris and detachment from social reality." Isn't this describing Gustav Graves?

The complex is perceived in the shape of pendulous emotion, ecstatic high and the depressive low of bipolar disorder. It is particularly apparent where a person is fond of heights, fascinated by both fire and water, narcissistic and obsessed with fantastical or far-fetched imaginary cognition. Coincidentally, one of the rumoured titles for Bond 20 was *Fire and Ice* before it became *Die Another Day*. Maybe this could go some way to explain the fantasy elements and stretching of reality - a car with adaptive camouflage, ice palace and CGI parasurfing a tsunami in the second half of the film. That too might be a stretch.

Casino Royale

You Know My Name:
Reintroducing an iconic character

"Well I understand Double-0s have a very short life expectancy."

The reboot of the Bond character by filming Fleming's first Bond book properly was an innovative move by Eon Productions. After twenty films and fifty-three years after the character's literary debut in 1953, this retcon was a successful cinematic concept and conceit, a gamble that seriously paid off. The prospect of introducing a character in 2006 with which the audience is already familiar may seem an impossible task. The title song, *You Know My Name*, reinforces the idea for the audience: we already know the name of this character. The teaser poster for the launch of *Goldeneye* did a similar but softer reboot in 1995 - *You Know the Name, You Know the Number* - reintroducing Bond to the silver screen with a new actor after the six year hiatus from *Licence to Kill*.

In *Casino Royale* we are to believe this is not the Bond that we know. Instead we go on a journey with him, witnessing him take on the mantles of his character and personality as the plot progresses. Ultimately, to the bars of the classic Bond theme, he becomes the character we can all recognise.

There is strong precedent for such a reintroduction long before *Batman Begins* released the previous year in 2005. Fifth Century BC Athens with its dramatic competitions and performances was full of playwrights reintroducing, reimagining and reinterpreting iconic mythical heroes for a contemporary audience. Use of the mythical past, particularly tales from the Trojan War were a tool for discussing present issues and referencing current affairs.

The dramatist Euripides exhibited this to a greater degree than his contemporary playwrights Aeschylus or Sophocles. For instance, in his play *Hecuba*, lines 131-132, Odysseus is represented as *"agile-minded, sweet-talking, demos-pleasing."* This resembled contemporary Athenians rather than the heroic figures of myth. He gave novel characteristics to heroic figures and was versatile in doing so. He could easily move between the tragic, the romantic and political effects.

This versatility is relevant in looking back at the different actors and different sorts of films that Eon have produced since *Dr No*. In order to keep their hero fresh, they keep up with the times and trends of cinema, setting Bond in the present rather than his literary roots in the 1950s and '60s. The scriptwriters lean into their leading men's strengths, whether it be the Shakespearean actor Timothy Dalton's more serious approach to the role, light-hearted tone with Roger Moore, the romantic suave sophistication of Pierce Brosnan or the more introspective Daniel Craig. We have today different Bond films for different moods, so broad is the template first set by the early Connery and Moore films. This keeps each of the films popular and relevant, as well as a cultural touchstone. This will also enable the series to continue again in the future.

There is another subtle classical reference in the film. The code *ellipsis* used by the terrorists and discovered by Bond to crack the security lock in Miami Airport means an omission of words or something that is left unsaid. It is also a punctuation device; one uses three dots (...) to signify this. So here this codeword represents the first half of the film, the modern set up for what is to follow which is not in Fleming's original novel, while the second half is a relatively faithful but modern adaptation.

Quantum of Solace

Aside from the meaning of the title, from the Latin word *quantum* - how much/degree - "A degree of comfort" in its reference to Bond overcoming his relationship with Vesper and the name of the evil organisation, there is little notable classical influence to the story.

However, what is worthy of comment is the development of the film and its link to the manner in which classical works were released. It is well known that Bond 22, *Quantum of Solace*, was already in development when *Casino Royale* was announced. Its original release date was May 2008 but then moved to October 2008. It was unfortunately a victim of a Hollywood writers' strike. Scriptwriter Paul Haggis, who had polished the script of *Casino Royale* so well, had to rush his script-doctoring of *Quantum of Solace*. Hence the production started with an unfinished script, leaving the director Marc Forster and actor Daniel Craig to make up lines on the hoof. "A writer I am not," Craig recalled.

The film was duly released to audiences and given mixed reviews as somewhat inferior to its illustrious predecessor *Casino Royale*. There are elements of merit to the film, individual scenes of style over substance. It is an elegantly shot film; it looks rich and clear. However, it is not generally regarded, even somewhat ignored, when set against the other Craig entries or the series as a whole.

In ancient literature there were works which were released before they were properly completed. The first century BC poet Virgil was still working on revising *The Aeneid* when he died in 19 BC. The poem contains a few lines which are only half as long as they should be. This confirms the traditional belief that the work is unfinished.

labor imperfectus?

However, there is a distinction between what is unfinished and what is incomplete. The emperor Augustus had commissioned Virgil to write a national epic poem for Rome. Virgil had worked on the project for eleven years and felt he had failed in his attempt to rival Greece's Homer's *Iliad* and *Odyssey*. He planned a three year trip to Greece and Asia to try to fix what he thought was wrong with *The Aeneid*. He died before he could finish. On his deathbed he had asked for his manuscript to be burned. Maybe he was just a perfectionist, because despite some shortcomings, the work is considered to be complete. In a similar way, *Quantum of Solace* may seem unfinished and rushed, with shortcomings, but it is a complete film.

The Aeneid's first line reads *"arma virumque cano"* - *"I sing of arms and of the man"*, as fitting for its hero Aeneas as it would be for Bond two millenia later. A key theme in the poem that Virgil explored is that of *pietas* - duty to gods, family and country. It is all about finding one's destiny, one's journey and the strength of Rome. Aeneas, a refugee from the fall of Troy, the legendary founder of Rome is almost comparable to James Bond who likes to see himself as outside the establishment and at the same time the epitome of Britishness.

Skyfall

"The inevitability of time, don't you think?"

Heroic hearts

The final lines of Alfred, Lord Tennyson's *Ulysses*, written in 1833 and published in 1842, is recited by M in a suitably dramatic moment. Voiced to a hero shot of Bond running through Westminster with Thomas Newman's rousing soundtrack, it contributes a lot to the thematic notes to the film as a whole:

> *Tho' much is taken, much abides; and though*
> *We are not now that strength which in old days*
> *Moved earth and heaven; that which we are, we are;*
> *One equal temper of heroic hearts,*
> *Made weak by time and fate, but strong in will*
> *To strive, to seek, to find, and not to yield.*

The poem is a popular example of dramatic monologue, with its main theme being the search for adventure and heroism. Ulysses, Odysseus in Greek, feels his old age but also the constant pull of adventure drawing him away from family and duty.

Old age is a knowingly explored theme of *Skyfall* by the filmmakers, celebrating fifty years of James Bond on the silver screen but also the relevance of Bond himself in the modern age of spying and cinema itself. There is a great deal of intertextuality.

In many ways, *Skyfall* is a modern day inspiration of Homer's *Odyssey*. It explores the themes of homecoming, *nostos*, the longing to return home and to family, the role of an aging hero, resurrection and rebirth, the conflict of a desire for one's own life and that of service, the awareness of one's mortality.

Written upon the death of his friend Arthur Henry Hallam, whom Tennyson had considered destined for greatness, the poet took influence from Homer's *Odyssey,* Dantes' *Inferno* and Shakespeare's *Trolius and Cressida*. He infuses Ulysses with a determination to defy age and circumstance. The parallel with an ageless James Bond is clear. Moreover, through the poem Ulysses has conflicting moods as he searches for continuity between his past and future, showing the strain, discontent and restlessness to push on. The film itself is serving as a marker of the legacy of films that have gone before and whatever may lie ahead.

The final line of the poem has often been used as a motto. However, with the film released in the same year as both the Queen's Diamond Jubilee and the summer Olympic Games in London, with the famous role of Bond himself in London 2012's opening ceremony, it was perhaps fitting that those words were also included on a wall in the athletes' village that year. And with Bond escorting Queen Elizabeth II, it is also worth noting that Tennyson served as Queen Victoria's poet laureate for many years. A patriotic choice on both counts.

Spectre

As longtime Bond fans would know from the early Bond films, the criminal organisation SPECTRE stands for *Special Executive for Counter-Intelligence, Terrorism, Revenge and Extortion.* However, this film uses the diminutive - *Spectre* - to signify another word for a ghost or phantom in the shadows, hence the dual meaning of the title with reference to the plot.

Images or likenesses of the dead would come back to serve a purpose in various forms of Greek tragedy. Aeschylus in particular used ghosts in his plays. They briefly come back to the land of the living for plot progression and to press the core messages of the plays. These ghosts would often be the deceased who were not buried with the right rituals or who suffered premature or untimely deaths, victims of violence including casualties of war. This lack of final fulfilment was sometimes so great that a ghostly spirit could appear among the living, set on revenge.

Daniel Craig's Bond fittingly first recognises a spectre from his past at the funeral in Rome. This incarnation of Blofeld - Bond's mentor Oberhauser's son - is a blast from the past and is indeed intent on revenge for Bond interfering in his nefarious plans.

Another spectre in the film is that of Mr White who shadowed Bond's movements in *Casino Royale* and now is a shadow of his former self. He is stricken with poison and is dying a slow death when Bond encounters him in Austria. He is now indeed the Pale King.

When Bond tracks Mr White's daughter Madeiline Swann, her father is a spectre to her, estranged as she is. The hotel *L'American* in Morocco drecks up ghosts of her parents' past life together. And for Bond, he finds the ghost of Vesper Lynd on a VHS marking her interrogation, which he throws down seemingly uncaringly in blunt contempt.

No Time to Die

The influence of Greek myth on the plot of *No Time to Die* is significant as is already clear, its use of the Heracles myth being the most obvious. However, there are even more links to Greek myth within the plot than you may think.

Bond and Swann are separated at the end of the pre-title sequence, much like Odysseus is separated from his wife Penelope by the Trojan War. Like the machinations of Blofeld coming between Bond and Swann, Poseidon commands the sea to take Odysseus off course. Bond has blinded a Cyclopean figure, Primo, much like Odysseus blinds the Cyclops in *The Odyssey*. In Euripides' satirical play *The Cyclops*, Polyphemus the Cyclops is shepherding his sheep in the hills of Etna; Primo orders the release of a herd of sheep to trap Bond's Aston Martin during the car chase in Matera, but in vain. The Italian setting is also a natural comparison.

The image of the goddess Britannia is prominent in the pre-title sequence and another echo of *On Her Majesty's Secret Service*.

When Bond in Jamaica is called back into action, we see him disembarking his yacht with a spear-gun. Is this a subtle nod to Poseidon, god of the sea? Later in the film Bond's blood is represented by the Greek letter *psi*. There is a patriotic nod to the trident, with the statue of Britannia in the title sequence. Nomi's symbol in the climax to the film is a Greek letter *phi,* which is the symbol for the golden ratio, a constant infinite number, which could also signal that 007 is constant regardless of Bond's fate in this adventure.

Swann's coyness about Mathilde being Bond's daughter is an allusion to Penelope and her hundreds of suitors in Odysseus' twenty years absence. This is the tragedy for Bond, the doubts over his fatherhood.

Swann is an allusion to the animal form (a swan) taken by Zeus when he fathered Helen with Leda, Queen of Sparta. Safin steals Swann much like Paris takes Helen of Troy, which is the cause of the Trojan War.

There are various similarities between characters in the film and characters from Homer: M as Agamemnon, Nomi as Calypso, Leiter as Patroclus, Bond as Achilles. Agamemnon behaves with arrogance and pettiness, losing the confidence of his best fighter Achilles as a result and sending the Greeks on course towards military disaster. The mood between M and Bond in the film is noticeably comparable. One can of course read too much into it and it may be as much about how storylines work and have just followed these tropes set by Homer from the beginning of Western literature. However, it is still fascinating to spot.

HMS Dragon is an allusion to Heracles' eleventh labour. Heracles had to slay the dragon Ladon to retrieve magical golden apples which bestow immortality, or "all the time in the world." Note that Bond gives apples to Mathilde for breakfast!

Heracles fights the Cyclops, as does Bond fight Primo, the one-eyed henchman, and, targeting his eye just as Odysseus does to the Cyclops Polyphemus. Heracles also defeats the Hydra, which could be considered SPECTRE-like. He equally finds himself poisoned by the Hydra's blood which contaminates one of his old shirts. This foreshadows Bond's own fate when he is contaminated by his contact with Madeline.

Epilogue

And so we end where we began. *No Time To Die* was a story pointing at the mortality of James Bond. Daniel Craig's films focused on the emotional deconstruction of the character. The producers have now tackled this head on from a beginning to end. It was everything or nothing.

Indeed this book started as a speculative article on the meaning of Bond's fate at the end of *No Time to Die*. It was a cathartic experience to get down my own thoughts to rationalise the ending and be content with it in my mind. Bond would no doubt be back cinematically, as promised at the end of the credits and is still out there as a fictional character.

Whether the filmmakers intended comparisons or not, it is interesting to investigate how story elements as much as story are timeless. The origins of such give us a greater understanding of ourselves as human beings and what inspired us, and what we can learn from in order to make progress. That is very much the purpose of studying Classics, beyond the buzz and natural high of translating an ancient text, for me at least.

I hope this comparative study of Bond and Classics will inspire you - to not only investigate these elements but also to be curious about Classics and find out more about the world of Bond. Whether it is picking up the Ian Fleming books or continuation novels or other areas, they can all open other areas of interest and make life more enriching.

Through researching and writing this *opus* I was surprised just how much morbidity and death there was, beyond the sex, violence, girls and guns. The filmmakers, the actors, the producers, the directors, the authors have all managed to find a root into exploring and cutting through the character's complexities. It is quite remarkable the appeal Bond still holds that his world has such diverse content and entertainment value.

Now is the world once again ready for its immortal hero to return on a mission, *in media res,* in the midst of his career? Or will we explore events before *Casino Royale?* What angle or tone will a relaunched series take? Whichever path is travelled, the focus will surely now be on what works best in the franchise's formula - the iconic bleeding gunbarrel, the loaded barrel of the Bond theme blazing, the Bond character himself, the villain, the women, the sex, the violence, the martinis, the action, the tension and suspense, a perfect cocktail to be shaken not stirred. The audience will be able to root once more for a man against the odds, their hero to save the day.

For Further Reading

Books

The Hero of a Thousand Faces, Joseph Campbell

The Oxford Companion to Classical Literature, edited by MC Howatson

The James Bond Bedside Companion, Raymond Benson

Some Kind of Hero: The Remarkable Story of the James Bond Films, AJ Chowdhury and Matthew Field

The Many Faces of James Bond, Mark Edlitz

James Bond After Fleming: The Continuation Novels, Mark Edlitz

James Bond: The Man and His World, Henry Chancellor

Ian Fleming: The Complete Man, Nicholas Shakespeare

When the Snow Melts: The Autobiography of Cubby Broccoli, Albert Broccoli with Donald Zec

Percy Jackson series, Rick Riordan

A Thousand Ships, Natalie Haynes

Amo, Amas, Amat…And All That: How To Become A Latin Lover, Harry Mount

It's All Greek To Me, Charlotte Higgins

The Greek Myths, Robert Graves

Mythos; Heroes; Troy; Odyssey, Stephen Fry

The Return of Ulysses, Edith Hall

The Hero: The Enduring Myth that Makes Us Human, Lee Child

Websites

https://www.007.com/

https://www.ianfleming.com/

https://www.mi6-hq.com/

https://classicsforall.org.uk/

Podcasts/YouTube Channels

James Bond Radio

Being James Bond

The Bond Experience

Bondcast

Acknowledgements

First and foremost to Ian Fleming for his creation, to Ian Fleming Publications and its commissioned authors; to Eon Productions, its cast and crews, its six Bond actors to date.

To my family who at first nurtured and subsequently tolerated my deep, borderline obsessive interest in Bond over the years. It has led to many other areas of interest and exploration in my life, not least in travel, open mindedness and the arts.

To my Classics Masters at RBAI and Durham University. Education pays the best dividend.

To all those in the Bond community, not least to Tom Sears and Chris Wright of *James Bond Radio*, David Zaritsky of *The Bond Experience* and Joseph Darlington of *Being James Bond* for hours of entertainment and film criticism, especially keeping me buoyant during the 2020-2021 pandemic.

To my editors and all those who encouraged my writing and for their thoughts and constructive feedback on bringing this to completion and publication.

JAMES BOND WILL RETURN

ADAM MUCKLE

• A BOND ODYSSEY •

Printed in Great Britain
by Amazon